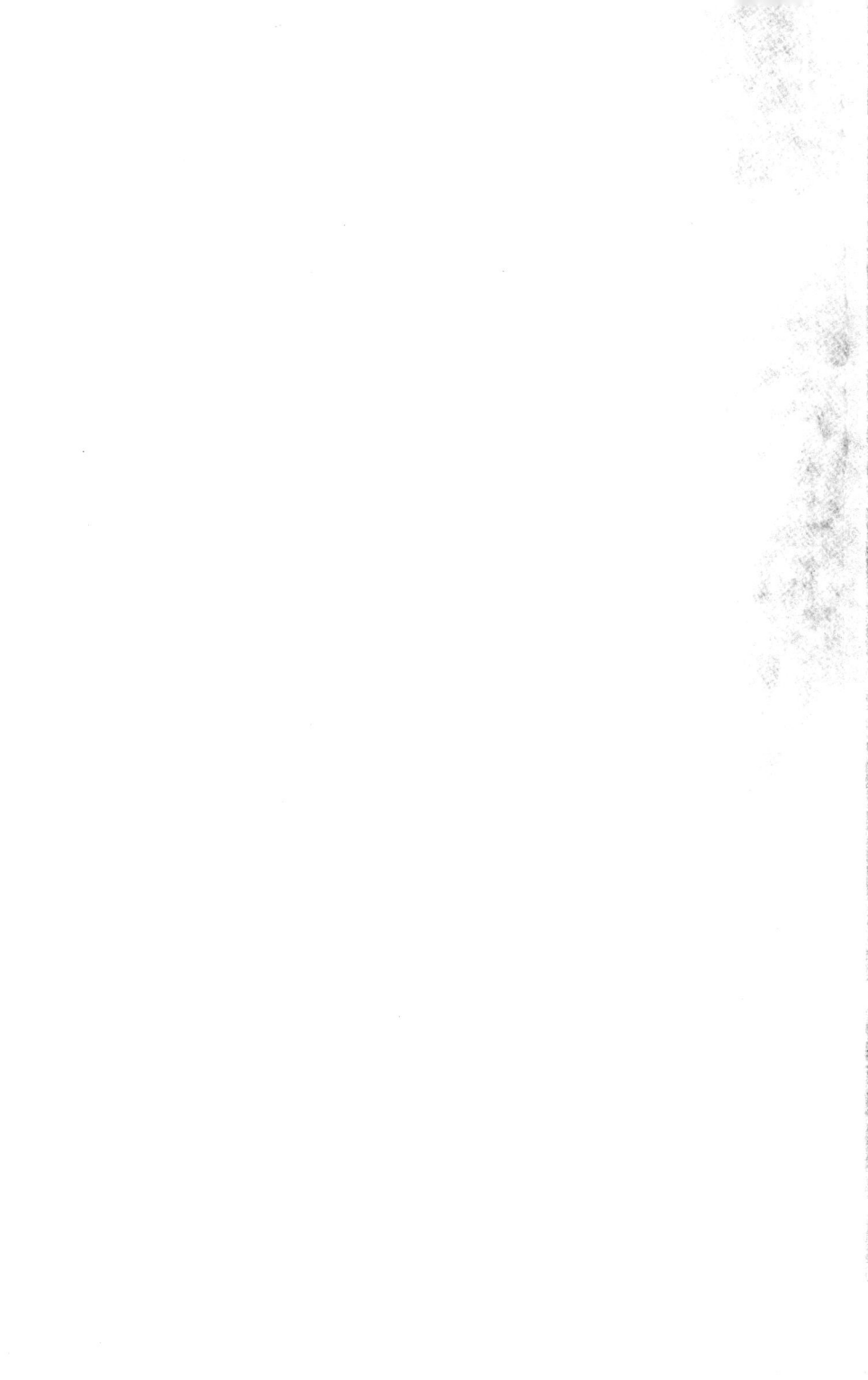

Humpty Dumpty

A Pantomime

Norman Robbins

Samuel French—London
New York – Sydney – Toronto – Hollywood

CHARACTERS

Mother Goose, fairy godmother to all
Jack Spratt, a village boy
Polly Flinders, his sweetheart
Tommy Tittlemouse, a village boy
Mary Quite Contrary, his sweetheart and ward of the
    King
Grimm, henchman to the Sorcerer
Dame Dobb, housekeeper to the King
Humpty Dumpty, a magical being
King Florimund XIV of Nursery-rhyme Land
Powder ⎫
Shott ⎬ two of the King's men
Monstro, The Sorcerer, a hunchbacked goblin of great
    size
Page
Little Bo-peep
Lake Monster
Chorus of **Nursery-rhyme Characters, Courtiers, Guests,
    Snow Spirits, Gypsies, Prisoners of Monstro,
    Clockwork Dolls, Pretty Maids and Gardeners,** and
    Guards
Babes chorus of **Palace Children, Nursery-rhyme Charac-
    ters, Pages in the Palace, Snow Spirits, Gypsy
    Children, Mice, Clockwork Dolls**

ACT I

ACT II

AUTHOR'S NOTE

Humpty Dumpty was first performed at the Grand Pavilion Theatre, Porthcawl, Mid Glamorgan, on December 26th, 1981, and directed by the author.

This version has been specially adapted for amateurs, but differs only slightly from the original. Staging has been simplified to suit the average church hall or small theatre, and lighting, special effects and properties kept to a minimum. Songs and dances are left to the discretion of the directors. The running time of the show is 2 hours 20 minutes, including a 12 minute interval.

For the sword fights in Act II, Scene 5, it is suggested that participants use fencing foils with button points for safety, and rehearse the fights most carefully.

The eggshell shards in Act I Scene 1 are easily made with tinted polystyrene tiles, broken into fairly large segments.

The Lake Monster is simply another version of the "Ghost" gag, but instead of a white sheet, a "tie-dye" one is used and bedecked with dark green and brown mesh, fish scales, claw hands and rubber fright mask. However, one can substitute with whatever is available, from the Incredible Hulk to the Frankenstein Monster.

Costumes and scenery should be as stylized as possible and the pace of the show brisk.

For
Liz and Dann Perkins
of Eau Claire, Wisconsin, USA
and
Margaret (Peggy) Murray
of Ames, Iowa, USA

With many thanks for all their hospitality
and friendship

ACT ONE*

Prologue

Mother Goose's Arbor

There is a gauze lane-cloth which depicts a gigantic shimmering spider's web. The Lights give the effect of early morning with, if possible, light mist

When the Curtain *rises Mother Goose is standing down* c, *smiling. She is dressed in the traditional costume of the nursery-rhyme character and carries a wooden spoon which she uses as a wand*

Mother Goose (*cheerily*)
　　　　　　　　Hello, my dears . . . and welcome
　　　　　　　　To the land of Nursery-rhyme.
　　　　　　　　I'm Mother Goose, your friend and guide
　　　　　　　　Throughout the pantomime.
(*She gives a deep curtsy before continuing*) Well, well, well. (*She peers around the audience*) You *are* a happy-looking audience. Not a gloomy face in sight. Mind you, I'm very glad to see it, because here in Nursery-rhyme Land we take a dim view of people with gloomy faces. In fact— to tell you the truth—it's even against the law. (*She nods gravely*) Oh, yes. There's *quite* enough misery and unhappiness in the mortal world without *us* having to put up with too. That's why we've decided that anyone in the audience caught scowling *or* sneering, will be banished from the theatre and sent to see (*names rival pantomime*) as a punishment. Right. Well now we understand each other, there's something I'd better tell you. Usually, there's nothing much to worry about in Nursery-rhyme Land, because as fairy godmother to everyone living here, *I* manage to keep a pretty sharp eye on things. However, according to *my* information, today looks like being a little *un*usual, and here's the reason. Right on top of the palace wall—overlooking the courtyard—is a huge EGG, held firmly in place by a magic spell and looking as if not even an earthquake could move it. Of course, *they've* no idea where it came from or even what it's doing there. All they *do* know, is that it's been up there for *centuries*, and seems to be some sort of lucky mascot. *They* call it Humpty Dumpty, and for the want of a better name, I think *we'd* better call it that too. (*She chuckles*) However, the magic holding it in place is fast running out and before very long will vanish completely. (*She nods wisely*) Well, we all know what will happen then, don't we? *Scrambled egg.* And all the King's horses and all the King's men, will *never* put Humpty together again. (*Brightly*) But not to worry. Everything that's going to happen has all been planned, and the Fairy Queen's put *me* in charge of making sure nothing goes wrong. There's plenty of

---

*N.B. Paragraph 3 on page ii of this Acting Edition regarding photocopying and video-recording should be carefully read.

magic left in my little wooden spoon if it should, but I don't think there's much chance of—(*She breaks off*) Ohoooo. We'd better be getting along to the royal courtyard. I've a funny feeling that things are starting to happen. Hold on to your seats and take a deep breath. I'm moving you there right *NOW*. (*She waves her wooden spoon*)

The Lights come up behind the lane-cloth to reveal the characters in position for Scene 1

Mother Goose exits as the lane-cloth flies out and the scene comes to life

Scene 1

The Courtyard of the King's Palace

A high-walled courtyard. There is a huge, well-lit egg perched c on the wall with a large arch l, through which part of the city can be seen. Sentry boxes stand either side of the arch. The palace is r and has a practical door

It is a bright, sunny morning and the people of Nursery-rhyme Land, led by Polly Flinders and Jack Spratt, are singing and dancing

SONG 1

Tommy Tittlemouse enters in a jaunty manner through the arch at the end of the song. He carries a simple kind of fishing rod over his shoulder and a short stick from which dangle several medium-sized fish

All greet him cheerfully and form a semi-circle about him as he moves c

Tommy (*brightly*) Hi, everybody. What do you think to *these*? (*He displays the fish*)

Polly So *that's* where you've been hiding yourself, Tommy Tittlemouse. Fishing in other men's ditches again.

Tommy (*unconcerned*) Well . . . I can hardly fish in my own, Polly Flinders, can I? There isn't a ditch for *acres* around *my* little house. (*He smiles*) But you don't have to worry. *This* time I had full permission. These little beauties are bound for the royal kitchens and King Florimund's dinner table.

Jack You don't mean to say he's having *fish* today, do you?

Tommy Why not? There's nothing wrong with a nice fat trout.

Polly But it's his *birthday*.

Jack You don't have *fish* on your *birthday*. You have venison . . . or pheasant . . . or thick, thick slices of best lean beef.

Tommy (*laughing*) That may be what *you* like Jack Spratt, but His Majesty particularly expressed a desire for a large plate of trout, and these are the best in the entire kingdom.

Polly (*looking at them*) Well . . . I must admit they're the best looking fish *I've* ever seen. Where on earth did you catch them? It couldn't have been anywhere around here.

Tommy You're right. As a matter of fact, they came from a big lake I found in the middle of the Great Forest.

All react in astonishment

Jack Don't say you've been wandering around *there* all on your own.

Polly (*protesting*) It's a horrible place. Full of witches, goblins and wolves.

Tommy (*laughing*) Maybe it is, but *I* didn't meet any. Besides, it was well worth the risk to land a catch like this. Now I can get myself into his good books before the party begins. I'm going to need all the help I can get tonight.

Jack (*amused*) I don't think *you've* anything to worry about, Tommy. Everyone in the kingdom knows that you and Mary are head over heels in love.

Tommy Everyone but King Florimund, you mean. What *he's* going to say when I turn up at the Ball asking permission to marry her, I can't imagine. After all, *she's* his royal ward, and *I'm* only a poor fisherman without a penny to my name.

Polly What does that matter? According to tradition, the King will grant the first three requests brought before him on the occasion of his Birthday Ball, and as far as *I'm* aware, no-one's ever ever been turned down.

All agree

Tommy (*wryly*) It'd be just *my* luck to be the first.

Jack (*scornfully*) There's about as much chance of *that* happening as there is of old Humpty there (*indicating the egg*) falling off the wall.

All look amused at the idea

Tommy (*brightening*) In that case I'd better start saving for a wedding ring, because I don't think he'll be taking a tumble *just* yet. If you ask me, he'll be perched up there till the end of time. Thanks for cheering me up. And now I'd better get these to Dame Dobb and see if I can steal a few minutes with Mary. I promised her I'd call this morning so I daren't keep her waiting.

Jack (*amused*) Hello. Got you under her thumb already, has she?

Tommy Certainly not. But you know how contrary she is. If I don't at least *try* to see her, she might change her mind about marrying me, and I don't think my nerves could stand it. Our secret engagement's been on and off twelve times this week already.

Everyone smiles

Polly Poor Tommy. She's my best friend, but she's so contrary I'm sure if she ever fell into the river, we'd have to search for her *up* stream.

Tommy Well, cheerio. Keep your fingers crossed for me tonight. (*He begins to move away towards the palace*)

Jack We'll do better than that. We'll all come along to give you encouragement.

Tommy (*delighted*) You will? Then if all goes well you can be guests of honour at the wedding.

All cheer, then Tommy joins them in a reprise of the opening song

SONG 1A (reprise)   No middle 8.

Jack, Polly and the people of Nursery-rhyme Land exit cheerily

Tommy turns once more to cross to the palace

As he does so, Mary Quite Contrary enters from the palace

Mary (*seeing him*) Tommy . . . (*She hurries to him*)

Tommy (*pleased*) Mary. I was just on my way to see you. Look at these. (*He displays his catch*)

Mary (*worried*) Oh, Tommy. I've got the most awful news. Tonight's party is going to be *cancelled*.

Tommy (*stunned*) But that's impossible. What on earth's happened?

Mary It's Uncle Florimund. He was having his daily fortune told by the court astrologer when suddenly a huge black bird flew in through the window and spoke to him.

Tommy What did it say?

Mary It was a piece of rhyme. "Birthday greetings here I bring. From Nursery-rhyme Land's future King. Before this day is out, my friend, your reign of peace will surely end."

Tommy (*scornfully*) What rubbish. Surely the King didn't take any notice?

Mary (*sadly*) I'm afraid he did. You see, when he asked the bird where it came from, it cried out: "From the castle of Monstro . . . King of all sorcerers", then flew out of the window. (*Worried*) Oh, Tommy . . . what are we going to do?

Tommy (*brightly*) Cheer up, Mary. I don't know who this Monstro is, but *I'm* certainly not afraid of him. Let him set foot in this part of the world, and he'll find he's got *me* to reckon with.

Mary But what about the Ball? Uncle Florimund is so upset that he's giving orders for it to be cancelled. If that happens, we won't be able to get married until *next* year.

Tommy You're right. We've got to get him to change his mind. (*He hands her the fish*) Look, you take these in to Dame Dobb, then see if you can talk him round. You know he'll do anything for *you*. I'll go find Mother Goose and tell *her* about all this. If anyone can help us, *she* can. Now don't worry. Everything will turn out all right. It always does in Nursery-rhyme Land, hadn't you noticed?

He squeezes her hand comfortingly, then exits through the arch

Mary stands there gazing after him, then as she turns to go back to the palace, her eyes fall on the egg

Mary (*brightening*) Of course. The egg. Now why didn't I think of that before? It's the answer to all our problems.

She exits quickly into the palace looking happy

As she does so the Lights dim

> *Grimm, the Sorcerer's henchman enters through the archway. He is all in black and as grim as his name. A green follow spot is directed on him throughout the play every time he appears*

Grimm (*looking around with a sneer*) So—this is the famous Land of Nursery-rhymes, is it? A perfect hunting-ground for my master, the Sorcerer. (*He leers*) And now to find a suitable victim. (*He begins to prowl around the courtyard*)

> *The palace door opens and Dame Dobb appears, singing cheerily*

Dame Girls were made to love and kiss, and who am I to interfere with this . . .?

Grimm (*turning*) Ahaaaaaaa.

Dame (*startled*) Blimey . . . It's Worzel Gummidge.

Grimm (*snarling*) Silence, you old hag.

Dame (*coyly*) Flatterer.

Grimm Do you know who I am?

Dame No. Surprise me.

Grimm (*puffing himself up*) I . . . am GRIMM.

Dame Grim? You're positively *gruesome*. Tell me . . . Is that your nose, or are you eating a banana? (*She suddenly realizes*) Just a minute. Just a minute. Did you say your name was Grimm?

Grimm (*sourly*) I did.

Dame (*to the audience*) Oh, boys and girls . . . Did you hear *that*? It's Grimm. *Grimm*. The *famous* Grimm. (*Ecstatically*) Oooooooh, I just *love* his fairy stories, don't you?

Grimm (*outraged*) *Fairy stories? Fairy stories?* I don't write fairy stories, you flannel-faced old faggot. I am henchman to the great Sorcerer, Monstro . . . King of *all* sorcerers.

Dame (*unconcerned*) Oh . . . well *I'm* Dame Dobb . . . housekeeper to King Florimund, and widow of this parish. (*She simpers at him, then realizes what he has said*) Eh? *Henchman to the Sorcerer?* Well what are you doing *here*?

Grimm (*leering*) My master sends me to find the prettiest, tenderest, *sweetest* young girl in this city, and carry her off to his enchanted castle where she will become—*his bride*.

Dame (*witheringly*) You wouldn't dare. (*Primly*) And besides . . . If you think *I'm* going to marry old Monstro, you've got another think coming.

Grimm (*amazed*) *You?* You, you bilious looking old bag of bones. I said I was looking for someone *pretty*. You're so ugly, if you went down to the docks, even the tug-boats would stop whistling.

Dame (*stung*) I resemble that remark, I do. For your inflammation, I've had lots of men at *my* feet.

Grimm (*sneering*) Really? Chiropodists, I presume?

Dame (*annoyed*) Right. That's done it. You've got ten seconds to get out of this courtyard in one piece. After that, you'll be leaving it in a box.

Grimm (*sneering*) You don't frighten me, you bottle-nosed old battle-axe. I could knock you to the ground with a single breath.

Dame I'm not surprised. It smells terrible. (*She wafts the smell away*) Do you *have* to eat garlic?

Grimm (*annoyed*) Fool. Dolt. Imbecile. Out of my way. (*He pushes past her and moves towards the palace*)

Dame (*dashing after him*) Here, not so fast, sparrow-legs. Just where do you think you're going?

Grimm (*scowling*) Into the palace, of course.

Dame (*running in front of him to stop him*) Over my dead body. You're not planting your dirty great plates of meat on my clean carpet. And besides, there's nothing in there that would interest *you*.

Grimm You think not? (*He leers*) Then what would you say if I told you I suspect that *somewhere* inside that building, the King's pretty young daughter may be hiding?

Dame I'd say you'd better go and do your suspecting somewhere else, because he hasn't *got* a pretty young daughter. In fact, he hasn't got any children *at all*. (*Smugly*) He's a bachelor, he is. Just the same as his father was.

Grimm (*snarling*) Bah! In that case I'll have to seek elsewhere for my master's bride. But remember . . . the *next* time I appear in this city, I shall expect its people to salute me in the manner I deserve. Understand? (*He turns away*)

Dame I certainly do. We'll have twenty-one guns ready to fire. And they'll all be *pointing* at you.

Grimm scowls, then exits through the arch

(*To the audience*) Oooh, boys and girls. What a nasty bit of work *he* is. I know we all sprang from monkeys, but if you ask me, *he* didn't spring far enough. What a face. I bet he has to creep up on the mirror to shave. (*Worriedly*) I'd better go warn King Florimund, just in case he comes back and tries to kidnap me. (*She thinks*) Mind you . . . *he's* worried enough to begin with. Perhaps I'd better wait till he's calmed down a bit. (*She sighs*) What a morning.

She exits into the palace

As she does so the Lights dim slightly

Mother Goose enters. She glances up at the egg

Mother Goose (*moving down c to speak to the audience*) Well, it's still up there, I see. It looks like the old spell has a bit of power left in it yet. But all the same:

Sooner or later, without any doubt,
The last scrap of magic is sure to run out;
And then, Humpty Dumpty, on top of that wall,
You're in, I'm afraid, for a terrible fall.
No hope of salvation—of merely a crack—

You're destined to shatter. They'll not put you back.
For though they may strive with their might and their main,
You'll never sit there on the coping again.

There is a low rumble of thunder and the Lights flicker gently. She quickly turns to look at the egg, then hurries upstage to stand below and to the left of it

The magic . . . It's going . . . It's going . . . It's gone.
There's nothing but gravity holding you on.
You're starting to rock from your base to your crown.
Look out, ev'rybody—*the egg's coming down.*

The thunder rises to a climax. The Lights flicker madly then Black-out. A great crash is heard and the thunder fades away into silence

Humpty Dumpty enters during the Black-out. The egg is removed and eggshell shards placed at the foot of the wall

There is a pause of a few seconds, then Humpty's voice is heard in the darkness

Humpty Ooooooooooooh? What happened? Where am I?

The Lights go up slowly to reveal Humpty Dumpty sitting at the foot of the wall, surrounded by shards of eggshell. He is dressed in a bright yellow costume. Mother Goose remains in the shadows, observing him

Oh, blimey. I'm down in the courtyard. I must have fallen off the wall. (*He glances up at it to measure the distance he fell*) Oooooh. (*He grimaces*) Thank goodness I landed on something soft. (*He rubs his head then suddenly sees the audience*) Oh . . . Hello. (*He scrambles to his feet and moves down* C *to speak to them*) Are you the *other* chickens? (*He peers*) Oh, yes . . . I can see one old boiler down there. (*He grins*) Oooh, isn't this a smashing little hen-house? There's one chicken at the back there holding a torch. I bet she's one of those battery hens they keep talking about. (*He points into the audience*) There's one down here sounds as though she's laying an egg. (*He beams*) Well, well, well. Look at all the happy faces. All enjoying yourselves, are you? (*Reaction*) Why? What are you doing? (*He laughs*) But honestly, aren't you glad you're here tonight instead of being at home watching television? Course you are. You know. I was on top of that wall when they invented television. I was. And do you know what the critics said about it? They said it was a *bad thing* because it would replace the *art of conversation.* They must have been mad. Television hasn't replaced the art of conversation. It's replaced *cleaning, ironing, washing* and *cooking.* (*He chortles with laughter*)

Mother Goose comes forward

Mother Goose Welcome to Nursery-rhyme Land, Humpty Dumpty.
Humpty (*turning to see her*) Ooooooh! It's (*well-known personality*).
Mother Goose (*smiling*) No, no, Humpty. I'm not (*repeats the name*). I'm
    Mother Goose, fairy godmother to all who live in this magical place—

and that includes *you*. It's my job to see that everyone needing help or advice, gets it.

Humpty In that case, thank goodness you've come, 'cos *I* need some help. You see, I've just fallen off that wall and smashed my shell, and I've no idea how I'm going to put it back together again. Can *you* do it for me?

Mother Goose (*shaking her head*) I'm afraid not, Humpty. Here you are, and here you must stay.

Humpty Well . . . it's all right *now*. I've made some smashing friends out there in the audience. But what if I decide later on that I'd rather be back in my shell? I can go back *then* can't I?

Mother Goose shakes her head, still smiling

Cor . . . some fairy godmother *you* are.

Mother Goose Don't be upset, Humpty. You won't be needing that old shell any more. From this moment on, there's a new life waiting for you. Two thousand years you've been sitting on top of that wall. Now it's time for you to start the task you were created for.

Humpty (*baffled*) Eh? What's that?

Mother Goose You'll find out, soon enough. But just for the moment, remember *this*. You, Humpty Dumpty, are a very special person. No-one else in the whole wide world has the power that *you* have. Anything you want can be yours—simply by *wishing* for it.

Humpty (*impressed*) Oooooooooh.

Mother Goose Just one warning. Use your gift wisely and nothing will be impossible for you; use it selfishly, and not only will you destroy your *own* happiness, you'll destroy that of everyone living in Nursery-rhyme Land *at the same time*. Do you understand?

Humpty But—but how will I know if I'm *being* selfish? I don't even know what selfish is. I mean . . . I've only just come out of an egg and I don't know *anything*.

Mother Goose (*nodding wisely*) That's very true, Humpty, so you've a lot of catching up to do, haven't you? Now remember what I've said and watch your step. (*She begins to exit*)

Humpty (*urgently*) Wait. Missis Duck. Don't leave me on my own. Not just yet.

Mother Goose Don't worry. I'll never be *too* far away from you. As a matter of fact, I'll be keeping an eye on you for the rest of your life. In the meantime—don't forget—whatever you wish for will be yours at once. No questions asked.

She exits quickly

Humpty (*calling after her*) But—but—you haven't told me what a wish *is*. How can I make one if I don't know what they look like? (*He slumps*) Oh, blimey. She's gone. Now what am I going to do? (*He looks around him*) Well . . . I don't suppose I'm expected to stand here all day. Perhaps I'd better go and have a look round. (*To the audience*) See you later, kids.

He moves uncertainly towards the rear of the palace and exits behind it.

Powder and Shott, two of the King's men, enter through the arch. They are
wearing uniforms and carry muskets (or swords), but look sloppy

Shott (*looking around with satisfaction*) Well, here it is, Powder. The
courtyard of the King's palace. Now, you know what we have to do?
We've to stop any suspicious looking strangers from skulking around.

Powder (*excitedly*) Cor . . . Isn't it exciting, Shott? Our very first day as
King's men, and here we are guarding the royal residence.

Shott (*swaggering down* C) Pooh. It's nothing to get worked up about.
After all, it's only a job like any other.

Powder (*following him*) Huh. You weren't saying that this morning when
we didn't know where the next meal was coming from, were you? We
hadn't eaten a thing since we got thrown out of the (*names local restaur-
ant*) four days ago.

Shott And who's fault was that, eh? It was yours. If you hadn't drawn
attention to us with your noisy eating, the manager wouldn't have found
out we were broke till after we'd finished.

Powder (*indignantly*) What do you mean, noisy eating? I'm not a noisy
eater.

Shott Oh, no? Then how come the minute you started guzzling your soup,
six couples got up to dance?

Powder Har, har. Very funny. At least *I* didn't show myself up by washing
my cutlery in the finger bowl.

Shott (*surprised*) What's wrong with that? You didn't expect me to put it
in my pocket with shepherd's pie all over it, did you?

Powder (*amazed*) In your *pocket*? You don't mean to say you actually
stole that cutlery?

Shott Well . . . yes. But I didn't mean to. I took it by mistake.

Powder Mistake? How can you pinch stainless-steel cutlery by *mistake*?

Shott Easily. I thought they were *silver*.

Powder Oooh, you ought to be ashamed of yourself, you do. Don't you
know what happens to people who steal from other people?

Shott Yes. They go to work for the Inland Revenue. (*He chortles, then
gives a yelp of pain and holds his cheek*) Owww.

Powder What's wrong?

Shott (*gingerly*) I've got toothache.

Powder Serves you right for stealing.

Shott (*groaning*) Oh, it's not funny. I'll have to go to the dentist's as soon
as I get off duty.

Powder Dentists? Dentists? You don't want to waste your money on
dentists. Listen. *I* had a toothache once, and all I did was to go round to
my girl-friend's house. She kissed me, stroked my cheek, hugged and
squeezed me, and in less than five minutes, the pain had gone. Now
why don't *you* try the same treatment?

Shott (*cheering up*) I think I will. Where does your girl-friend live?

Powder (*pushing him in annoyance*) Oooh, I don't know why I put up with
you, I really don't.

Shott I can tell you *that*. It's because whenever it comes to brain-power, *I*

have to do all the work. You're so stupid that you have to stand on your head to turn something over in your mind.

Powder (*indignantly*) That's a lie. I'm very intelligent, I am. When I was at school, I was the teacher's pet.

Shott Yes. She kept you in a cage at the back of the classroom.

Powder (*stung*) All right. All right. I'll prove it to you. Ask me a question. Anything you like. I'll show you whether I've got brains or not.

Shott Right. What did Julius Caesar say when Brutus stabbed him?

Powder Er . . . (*He thinks*) I know: "Ouch."

Shott (*triumphantly*) You see? You're as thick as two short planks. He didn't say "Ouch." He said—(*with great drama*)—"*Et tu, Brute.*" (*He looks smugly at Powder*)

Powder (*unconvinced*) I bet he said "Ouch" first, though. Go on. Ask me another.

Shott All right, then. I'll give you an *easy* one. Name me five things that contain milk.

Powder (*laughing*) Five things that contain milk. Simple. (*He ticks them off on his fingers*) Butter . . . cream . . . cheese . . . (*he thinks a moment then says triumphantly*) . . . and two cows.

Shott (*disgustedly*) I give up. It's perfectly obvious you don't know anything. You're about as much use as an empty stewpot is to a cannibal.

Powder (*puzzled*) What's a cannibal?

Shott (*amazed*) What's a cannibal? (*Patiently*) Look, I'll try to explain it as simply as I can. Suppose that *you* had just finished eating your mother and father for dinner.

Powder Yes.

Shott Now what would that make you?

Powder (*light dawning*) Oh . . . an orphan.

Shott turns away with a groan

Mary enters from the palace and sees them

Mary Oh. (*She crosses to them*) Excuse me, but are you the new guards?

Shott (*turning to see her*) Eh? Oh . . . er . . . yes, miss. Powder and Shott, at your service.   SONG 2

The men try to tidy themselves up

Mary I'm so glad I found you. His Majesty wants to speak to you at once.

Powder (*pleased*) Oooh. Here . . . he's not going to promote us already, is he?

Mary (*laughing*) I'm afraid not. But I've managed to persuade him not to cancel his party tonight, so he wants to give you both some new orders. You'd better hurry along. He's not in the best of moods today because of his foot, so it wouldn't be wise to keep him waiting. (*She indicates the door to the palace*) It's through that door and the tenth turning on the right.

Powder and Shott exit quickly

Oh, thank goodness I remembered that little rhyme about the egg. (*She*

quotes) "While e'er the egg stays on the wall, the royal crown will never fall." (*Hugging herself*) I can't wait to tell Tommy. (*Sighing*) Oh, if only it were evening now and we were waiting for the Ball to begin. It'll be hours before he gets back, I suppose. It really *is* unkind of Father Time to move so slowly.

SONG 2

After the song, Mary quickly exits into the palace again, still not seeing the fragments of the egg

Humpty enters down R

Humpty Hiya, kids. Well—I've had a look round this part of Nursery-rhyme Land and it doesn't look *too* bad. All I've got to do now is to meet a few of the people and see what *they're* like. (*Sighing*) Oooooooh. I wish I could make a start with somebody.

There is a flash and Tommy appears

(*Startled*) Oooooooh. It's a feller that's lost his trousers.

Tommy (*bewildered*) How did I get here? (*He turns and sees Humpty*) And who are *you*?

Humpty I'm Humpty Dumpty.

Tommy Humpty Dumpty? (*He grins*) Well—you're certainly dressed in the right colour. (*He indicates the wall behind him without looking*) I suppose you came off the top of that wall, eh?

Humpty That's right. I felt tired and *dropped off*.

Tommy (*laughing*) In that case I expect your brains must be feeling a bit *scrambled*?

Humpty Oh, I'm all right now, but when it first happened, I was *shattered*.

Tommy (*highly amused*) Shattered. (*He suddenly catches sight of the broken shell and sobers up*) Oh, my goodness. (*He looks up at the empty wall*) I don't believe it. (*He stares at Humpty*) You *are* the egg. (*Calling urgently*) Quick everybody. Quick. Your Majesty. There's been a terrible accident.

Humpty stands bewildered

People, including Mary, Polly, Jack, Powder and Shott, tumble on to the stage in breathless excitement. Cries of "What is it?", "What's happening?" etc. are only silenced when a loud fanfare is heard. All fall back

A Page appears in the palace doorway

Page (*proclaiming*) His Royal Majesty, King Florimund the Fourteenth. King of all Nursery-rhyme Land.

All but Humpty bow and curtsy

The King enters from the palace. He is in full regalia and sports a heavily-bandaged foot. He looks annoyed

King (*coming down* C) What is it? What's all the commotion?

Tommy Look, Your Majesty. (*He points at the shattered shell*)

King (*seeing it*) Oooo-er.

Tommy And look what came out of it. (*He indicates Humpty*)

All stare at Humpty who looks most uncomfortable

King This is terrible. Quick. Somebody fetch the Sellotape. We've got to get him back on the wall *at once*.

Humpty (*startled*) Eh? Here—hang on a minute. I'm not going back inside that thing. I've only just come out.

King (*annoyed*) You'll do as you're told. You've caused enough trouble already. Unless you go back to where you belong, I'm going to lose my crown.

Humpty Never mind your silly old crown. If I go back inside that shell, I'm going to lose my marbles. I've been stuck in there for the last two thousand years with nothing to eat but egg yolk. Now I'm down here, I'm going to stay down.

King (*firmly*) Oh, no you're not. (*Loudly*) Call out my horses and call out my men. We're going to put Humpty together again. (*He stamps his bad foot*) Owwwwwww!

Mary (*stepping forward*) Uncle Florimund—wait. I'm sure there's nothing to get excited about. (*She crosses to Humpty*) He doesn't look dangerous to *me*. (*She smiles at Humpty*)

Polly Or me. (*She steps forward and waves to Humpty*) *I* think he's rather sweet.

Jack pulls her back into line with a frown

King Sweet? Sweet? You don't know what you're saying, child. Everyone knows the legend as well as I do. If the egg falls down, I lose my crown. So long as he's running around loose, we could *all* be in danger. He may even have been conjured up by the Sorcerer.

All react and move back

Jack The King's right.

Mary (*scornfully*) What nonsense. You've only got to look at him to see that he wouldn't hurt a fly. Poor Humpty . . . (*She hugs him*) Silly King Florimund doesn't know what he's talking about, does he?

King (*startled*) *What?*

Tommy (*perplexed*) Mary . . .

Mary (*tartly*) And as for *you*, Tommy Tittlemouse, how you can stand there and listen to all this without trying to defend the darling little creature, I'll never know.

King (*groaning*) Oh, no. She's gone all contrary again.

Mary (*grabbing Humpty's hand*) Come along, Humpty. I'll look after you.

Tommy Now just a minute . . . (*He steps in front of them*)

Humpty (*smiling*) I'm going with her, now.

King (*annoyed*) This is all *his* fault. (*He points at Humpty*) Guards. Arrest that object.

Powder and Shott hurry forward and grab Humpty

Now then. Get up on that wall *at once.*

Powder and Shott release Humpty and head for the wall

No, no, no. Not you, you fools. Him.

They hurry back looking sheepish

(*Prodding Humpty*) Quickly, or I'll make you wish you'd never set *foot* in this courtyard.

Humpty (*gulping*) I'm wishing that *now.* I wish I was miles away.

There is a flash and an instant Black-out, followed by sounds of confusion

Humpty exits in the darkness

The Lights come up again

Polly (*looking around*) He's gone.
Jack Vanished into thin air.

All react in fear and astonishment

King (*worriedly*) Sound the alarm at once. We've got to find him before it's too late.

Everyone, except for the King, Mary and Tommy, exits quickly

Mary (*smugly*) Well it jolly well serves you right, and I hope you *never* catch him. Poor little man. He was *so* nice . . . And you two were simply *horrible* to him.
Tommy Mary . . .
Mary (*sharply*) Don't speak to me. I never want to see either of you again.

She flounces off

Tommy (*distressed*) Oh, no. (*Calling*) Mary . . . wait.

He hurries out after her

King (*groaning*) Oh, dear. What a birthday this is turning out to be. Whatever's going to happen now?

He totters weakly towards the palace as the Lights fade to Black-out

SCENE 2

The Edge of the Great Forest. A leafy glade

Humpty enters looking downcast

Humpty (*without much enthusiasm*) Hiya, kids. (*He sighs*) Cor . . . what a rotten place Nursery-rhyme Land's turned out to be. I've only been out of my shell five minutes, and already that King Florimund's trying to get me put back inside it. Some "new life" this is. Here I am . . . a poor innocent little egg . . . all alone in a strange new world . . . and I

haven't got a single friend. Not one. Oohhhhhhhh. (*He suddenly brightens*) Here—just a minute, though. That Mary was quite nice, wasn't she? I bet *she'd* be my friend if I asked her, don't you? (*Excitedly* Shall I? Shall I ask her? All right, then. (*He closes his eyes*) I wish—I wish that Mary was right here with me.

There is a flash and Mary appears

Mary (*startled*) Oh . . .
Humpty (*gleefully*) It worked. It worked.
Mary (*turning to see him*) Humpty.
Humpty Hello, Mary.
Mary (*looking around*) What on earth am I doing out here?
Humpty (*happily*) I brought you here with one of my magic wishes.
Mary (*taken aback*) Oh, you did, did you? (*Annoyed*) Well you can jolly well use *another* of them and send me right back to where I came from. (*She stamps her foot angrily*)
Humpty (*startled*) But—but—I wanted to ask you something.
Mary (*not interested*) Oh?
Humpty (*almost afraid to speak*) I—I wanted to ask you if—if you'd be my friend. You see—I haven't got a friend in the world, and you were so nice to me when I fell off the wall.
Mary (*still annoyed*) That was only because almost everyone else was so nasty. *I* always have to be different. That's why I'm called Mary Quite Contrary.
Humpty (*sadly*) Oh. I didn't know that. (*He hangs his head and begins to move away*)
Mary (*her mood changing*) Humpty—wait.

Humpty turns as she runs to him

I've just remembered. The King and all his men are still looking for you, so that means it will be *perfectly* all right to be your friend.
Humpty (*delighted*) Honest?
Mary (*hugging him*) Oh, Humpty. I'm *so* sorry I was beastly to you. From now on I'm going to be the best friend you'll ever have.
Humpty (*squirming with glee*) Ooooooooooooh!
Mary Now let's see. First of all, we've got to find somewhere for you to live. (*She thinks*) I know. Down at the end of this path is the cottage that once belonged to the Old Woman Who Lived In A Shoe. It'll be the *perfect* place. Come on. I'll take you there. (*She takes his hand*)
Humpty Cor—what a smashing day it's turned out to be after all. I've got *magic powers*, and *you* for a friend. What else could an egg wish for?
Mary (*laughing*) I don't know . . . but whatever it turns out to be, you can bet your life *I'm* going to be helping you to get it. After all, that's what friends are for.

They sing

At the end of the song they exit happily, hand in hand

Grimm enters opposite in a temper

Grimm (*snarling*) Bah. Are there *no* pretty girls in this idiotic country? The only ones *I've* seen look worse than their passport photographs. How can I return to my master without a bride for him? I must look again and . . . (*He glances off*) Wait—someone's coming this way. (*He peers off*) A female, too. (*He leers*) I'll hide behind a tree and surprise her.

Grimm scuttles off to hide

As he does so, Dame Dobb enters opposite wearing an outrageous costume with a very low neckline

Dame Hello, girls and boys. Do you like the frock? (*She smiles*) Made it myself. It's called the "Bingo" style. Eyes down, and look in for a full house. (*She chortles*) Oh, but I love clothes, don't you? I spend all my spare money on them. I've got *one* dress that's so low cut, one false move and the men'll appreciate it. (*She shrugs*) Well—if you've got a good figure, you might as well show it, mightn't you? Still, I don't know why I'm going on about clothes. I've just walked out here for a bit of peace and quiet. Oh, that *palace courtyard*. Everybody dashing about with tubes of glue, trying to stick the egg back together. Old Florimund chewing his fingernails. (*She sighs deeply*) Oh, what a worrier that man is. And timid with it. Do you know, he won't even open an *oyster* without knocking on the shell first. It's no wonder the palace children call him King Jigsaw. You've only got to shake him up and he falls to pieces. Mind you, I wouldn't mind a few of the pieces coming in *my* direction. Ooooooh, what a body that man's got. I think it must be something to do with his weight-lifting. He's at it all the time, you know. Last year, he even entered a competition for it. Believe this or not, he lifted *two tons* in one straight thrust. Just like this. (*She illustrates lifting*) He won the title outright. He's now known as the world's most perfectly ruptured man. Still, I've got to admit it, he's exactly the kind of man I'd like to marry. He's alive. I've been trying to get him to notice me for years, but without avail. (*She thinks*) Perhaps I should try wearing one?

Tommy enters looking very downcast

Of course, the obvious thing to do is to . . . (*She notices Tommy and frowns*) Hey—Tommy. Come here. Come here.

Tommy comes to a halt and turns sadly

What on earth's the matter?

Tommy Oh, Dame Dobb. It's Mary. She told me she never wanted to speak to me again, and ran off. I've been looking everywhere for her, but she's vanished without trace.

Dame (*kindly*) Oh . . . don't get all upset about it, Tommy. She'll change her mind again soon. You know what she's like.

Tommy But what if she doesn't? We *were* going to ask the King's permission to get married tonight.

Dame (*startled*) Eh? Oh, well . . . in that case, we'd better try something drastic. Why don't you ask Mother Goose to help you find her?

Tommy (*brightening*) Of course. Why didn't *I* think of that? (*He calls*) Mother Goose.

Dame (*calling*) Mother Goose. Goosey, Goosey.

Mother Goose enters. She holds a stem rose

Tommy (*eagerly*) Oh, please, *please* help me. Mary's gone all contrary again, and I can't find her anywhere.

Mother Goose (*smiling*) Don't worry, Thomas. She'll be along in a minute. In fact, here she comes now. (*She indicates off with her spoon*)

Tommy (*relieved*) Thank goodness for that. But—but she said she wouldn't speak to me.

Mother Goose Here. (*She hands him the stem rose*) Take this magic rose. Wave it under her nose, and she'll be back to normal in no time. Just you see.

She crosses and exits

Dame (*wide eyed*) Well, I never. (*She thinks*) Mind you . . . I think I did a couple of times.

Mary enters, nose in the air

Tommy (*stepping in front of her*) Mary . . .
Mary (*tossing her head*) Don't speak to me.

Tommy waves the rose under her nose

Ohhh. (*She blinks and shakes her head to clear it*) Tommy. What a lovely surprise. Oh, I *am* glad to see you. (*She hugs him*) Wherever have you been? (*Eagerly*) Come on. Let's go back to my cockle-shell garden and talk about our wedding plans.

Tommy beams with delight, drops the rose, and taking Mary's hand, exits with her

Dame (*amazed*) It worked. It really worked. (*She thinks*) Hmmm. I wonder if it'll work for anybody? (*She simpers*) I'll try it out on the next man to come along. (*She picks it up*)

King Florimund enters dejectedly

King (*to himself*) Oh, dear, oh, dear. What a terrible birthday I'm having. What on earth are we going to do? The egg won't go back on the wall, and the Sorcerer's henchman can't be found anywhere.

Dame (*coyly*) Yoo-hoo. Florimund. (*She wiggles her fingers at him*)
King (*uninterested*) Oh, hello, Dame Dobb.

Dame My, my. You *have* got a long face today, haven't you? Oh, come on. Cheer up. I know things are bad, but they're not *that* bad. I'll tell you what. Come over here and give me a great big kiss. (*She puckers her lips at him*)

King (*startled*) I beg your pardon?

Dame (*moving in to him*) Well don't look so surprised. After all, *you're* a bachelor and *I'm* a widow. There's a lot of folk who think it's high time we got married.

King I suppose it is . . . but who'd have us?

Dame (*patiently*) I mean, wouldn't *you* like to marry *me*?

King *You*? Oh, no, my dear. I couldn't possibly marry *you*. Look at the difference in our ages.

Dame Pooh, that's nothing to worry about. Everybody tells me I get younger every day.

King Well that's true enough. You were fifty ten years ago, and now you're forty-four. (*Firmly*) No, no, Dame Dobb. It's quite out of the question.

Dame But—but—you can't be turning me down because of my *looks*, can you? I mean—I've still got *those*. (*With drama*) Oh, it may sound like vanity—but I can sit for hours, gazing at my beautiful reflection in the mirror.

King (*kindly*) That's not vanity, my dear—it's imagination.

Dame (*put out*) Oh, shut up and sniff this. (*She pokes the rose under his nose*)

King (*blinking*) Ohhhhh. (*Dreamily*) What a beautiful aroma. How exquisite. (*Puckishly*) But not half as exquisite as *you*, my little lollipop. (*He pinches her bottom*)

Dame (*jumping*) Ouch. (*She rubs her bottom*) It worked. It worked.

King (*slipping an arm around her waist*) Come back to the palace with me, you adorable creature, you.

Dame (*swooning*) Oh, did you hear *that* girls? He called me his adorable creature. (*She suddenly sobers*) Ah . . . but hold on a minute. (*To the King*) It's all right you calling me that *now*, but will you still be saying it when I'm old and ugly?

King (*gallantly*) My angel. You may grow older, but in my eyes, you could never grow uglier.

Dame Dobb double-takes, then is swept off by the King, dropping the rose as she exits

Grimm emerges from hiding

Grimm I wouldn't have believed it if I hadn't seen it with my own eyes. (*He snatches up the rose*) I must try it out at once. 'Twill make my task a thousand times easier.

A Pretty Girl enters

She crosses the stage and Grimm waves the rose under her nose

Girl (*annoyed*) How dare you, you revolting-looking creature. Take that. (*She slaps his face*)

She exits in a huff

Grimm (*reeling*) What happened? What did I do wrong?

Humpty enters

Humpty Here—I *saw* that. She hit you, didn't she?
Grimm Yes. But I don't understand why. I did exactly the same as the others.
Humpty What was that?
Grimm This. (*He waves the rose under Humpty's nose*)
Humpty (*blinking*) Ohhhh. You sexy-looking hunk of man. Quick. Give me a kiss.

Grimm reacts in horror and dashes off, chased by Humpty

Black-out

SCENE 3

Mary's Cockle-shell Garden

An old-fashioned, English country garden, containing hollyhocks, lupins, etc. with silver bells tied to tree branches and flowerbed borders edged with cockle-shells

The Lights come up to give a silhouette effect. Polly and Jack are down L, *Tommy and Mary are* C, *and a small rustic bench is down* R. *All the Girls of the chorus are in the background and all the boys, dressed as Gardeners, are positioned about the set. All the characters are "frozen"*

All (*singing*) Mary, Mary, Quite Contrary,   Song 3
                   How does your garden grow?
Mary (*singing*) With silver bells, and cockle-shells,
                     And pretty maids all in a row.

The Lights come up to full as the figures come to life and begin to sing and dance

~~SONG 4~~

After the song, the Choristers fall back leaving the others C

Polly Oh, Mary, we're *so* glad you're back to normal again.
Mary Me too. I can't *think* why I'm so contrary. I *do* try not to be, honestly I do.
Tommy We know. But to be perfectly fair, it wasn't all *your* fault, was it? That Humpty Dumpty was as much to blame as anyone.
Mary (*stiffly*) Oh?
Jack Tommy's right. Everything was fine until *he* turned up. If you ask me, he's a menace to the kingdom. For all *we* know he *may* have been conjured up by Monstro.
Polly (*ruefully*) That's true. Look at the way he vanished when King Florimund tried to have him arrested.
Mary (*getting annoyed*) And wouldn't *you* have done the same if *you* had magic powers? Poor little man. Locked inside that smelly old egg for two thousand years, and the moment he gets out, everyone wants him to go back in again.

Everyone looks at her in surprise

Tommy Mary . . .

Mary Well for your information, Humpty happens to be *my* very special friend, and I won't hear a word said against him. If you're going to be horrible, you can all go away and be horrible somewhere else, thank you very much. (*She flounces away*)

Tommy But Mary . . . (*He follows her*)

Mary (*coldly*) If you can't be friends with him, you needn't bother to be friends with me.

Tommy Friends? But, Mary—we're much more than *friends*, surely. *We're* going to be married.

Mary (*sticking her nose in the air*) Are we, indeed?

Tommy Well of course we are . . . (*Apprehensively*) Aren't we?

Mary (*firmly*) Certainly not.

Polly Oh, please. Please don't say that, Mary. (*She runs to her*) Don't change your mind *again*.

Jack We didn't realize Humpty meant so much to you.

Mary He *doesn't* mean so much to me. (*Shaking her head as if to wake up*) He doesn't mean *anything* to me. It's Tommy I'm in love with.

Tommy (*relieved*) Thank goodness for that.

Mary (*bemused*) Oh, what's the matter with me? Why am I so contrary? One minute I want to get married, and the next, I can't bear to think about it. If only I could make up my mind like everyone else.

SONG 5

Tommy Never mind, Mary. I'm sure we all love you exactly as you are. I know *I* do. But just to be on the safe side, I think we'd better promise not to pass judgement on Humpty until we know a little bit more about him.

Jack Here, here.

Polly (*looking off*) Look. Here he comes now.

Mary (*startled*) Oh. (*She recovers herself*) Quick, everyone. Out of sight. If he sees a crowd, he may think we're trying to catch him, and disappear again.

The Gardeners and Girls quickly exit

A moment

Humpty enters

Humpty (*to the audience*) Hiya, kids.

Mary (*smiling*) Hello, Humpty. Welcome to my cockle-shell garden.

Humpty (*beaming*) Here, you'll never guess what I've been doing. I've been looking all around the city.

Jack Oh? And what do you think to the old place?

Humpty It's beautifully laid out, isn't it? I don't know when it died, but it's beautifully laid out. (*He chuckles*) But there's some very funny people living here, aren't there?

Polly How do you mean?

Humpty Well, I saw one man going down the street stealing all the garden gates.

Tommy And didn't you stop him?

Humpty Oh, no. I didn't like to say anything in case he took offence. (*He chuckles*)

Mary (*laughing*) Humpty. (*She takes his arm*) Meet my friends, Polly Flinders and Jack Spratt.

They greet each other

And this is Tommy Tittlemouse, the boy I'm going to marry.

Humpty (*delightedly*) Oooooooooh! (*To the audience*) Hey, did you hear that? The boy she's going to marry. (*To Polly and Jack*) She's going to marry him. (*To Mary*) You and him. Married. (*He frowns*) What's "marry"?

Tommy (*surprised*) Well—it's when two people love each other and want to be together for the rest of their lives.

Humpty (*eagerly*) Here—does that mean *I* can get married, then?

Jack Of course it does. Anybody can.

Polly (*puzzled*) But who do you want to marry? We didn't think you knew anybody.

Humpty I want to marry Mary.

Tommy (*laughing*) Now just a minute. We can't *both* marry Mary.

Humpty Why not? I'm in love with her, just as much as you are.

Mary Poor Humpty. You don't understand, do you? You haven't been out of the egg long enough. I can't possibly marry you, because it would be quite against the law to have two husbands.

Humpty No it wouldn't. It says in the wedding service, you can have sixteen.

Jack Sixteen?

Humpty Yes. Four better, four worse, four richer and four poorer.

All laugh

Mary Never mind, Humpty. I may not be able to marry you, but I'll always be your friend.

Polly And there are plenty of pretty girls left in Nursery-rhyme Land. All you have to do is look around until you find one.

Tommy Yes. But now we really have to be going. There's lots of things I want to discuss with Mary before the party begins.

Jack And there's one or two things *I* want to discuss with Polly. (*He puts his arm around her*)

Mary Cheer up, Humpty. We'll all see you later. Promise. (*She blows him a kiss*)

Mary, Tommy, Polly and Jack exit

Humpty (*disgruntled*) Huh. Left on my own again. Nobody to talk to and nowhere to go. I might as well have stayed in my shell for all the excitement I'm having. (*Suddenly*) Here—I know. Why don't I use one of my

wishes to find somebody *I* could get married to? (*To the audience*) Shall I do that, kids? Shall I? All right, then. (*He closes his eyes*) I wish—I wish there was somebody here who wanted to get married.

There is a flash and Dame Dobb appears

Dame Ooooh. Where am I?

Humpty (*opening his eyes*) Blimey. It's (*well-known personality*).

Dame (*seeing him*) Here—who are you? And what are you doing in this private garden?

Humpty I'm Humpty Dumpty—and I'm looking for someone to marry.

Dame Looking for someone to marry? You must be off your rocker. You won't find anybody round here who'd . . . (*She realizes*) Ohhhh. (*Quickly strikes a pose and preens herself*) Well *I'm* here.

Humpty (*looking her up and down*) *You?*

Dame Why not? There's many a good tune played on an old fiddle, you know. And I'll tell you something else. The man who marries me will get himself a prize.

Humpty (*curious*) What is it?

Dame It's *me*, you fathead. Can't you recognize beauty when you see it? (*Smugly*) You don't get looks like these by accident, you know. (*She touches her face*)

Humpty (*aside*) No. Only by being involved in one.

Dame (*not hearing*) My first husband used to tell me I looked like an angel that had fallen from above.

Humpty (*aside*) Yes. But it's a pity you had to land on your face.

Dame Mind you, I always *did* say my face was my fortune.

Humpty Well if that's true, I bet you don't have to pay much income tax. (*He chortles*)

Dame (*annoyed*) I *heard* that.

Humpty Oh, I'm only joking. Actually, you're rather nice, really.

Dame (*flattered*) I suppose I am. But then so are you. In fact the minute I laid eyes on you I thought, "Oh, I don't know who he is, but he does remind me of my third husband."

Humpty *Third husband?* How many husbands have you *had*?

Dame Two. (*With great feeling*) Oh, Humpty, now that we're finally engaged, will you promise to give me a ring?

Humpty Course I will. What's your number?

King Florimund enters and sees them

King Ooh, it's him. Quick, quick. Surround him. Guards.

Powder, Shott, Polly, Jack, Tommy, Mary and a crowd of Nursery-rhyme Land people enter

Arrest that object and put him back inside the egg at once.

Powder and Shott grab Humpty

Dame (*startled*) No. Wait. Florimund, what's happening?

King I'll tell you what's happening. (*He indicates Humpty*) That is the

henchman of Monstro the Sorcerer. Hatched from the giant egg to steal my crown and destroy the kingdom.

All react in various ways

Dame (*stunned*) Ohhh. And to think he nearly tricked me into marrying him. I could . . . (*She realizes*) Here—hold on a minute. This isn't the Sorcerer's henchman. That's a feller called Grimm. I met *him* in the courtyard this morning before all the excitement began.

King (*startled*) What?

Dame Yes. I was going to tell you about him as soon as you'd cheered up a bit.

King Well what did he look like?

Dame The first husband of a widow.

King (*indicating Humpty*) Then he isn't anything to do with Monstro, at all?

Humpty Of course I'm not. I'm just a poor little egg who's fallen out of his shell, and nobody seems to want me. (*He sniffles*)

Mary (*hurrying to him*) Poor Humpty. (*She comforts him*)

King But what about the legend? *And* his magic powers?

Tommy (*suddenly*) Of course. I can see it all, now.

King reacts and tries to cover himself

Humpty's been sent to help us.

Polly Help us?

Tommy Don't you see? For two thousand years the egg sat on top of the courtyard wall because we were never in any danger. But now Monstro threatens to destroy our happiness . . .

Jack (*catching on*) The egg's fallen off the wall and Humpty's come out of it to protect us.

Everyone reacts

Mary Oh, Humpty. I knew they were all wrong about you. (*She hugs him*)

Powder Just a minute. *Him*—protect *us*? That's a laugh.

Shott You've only to look at him to see how much help *he'd* be.

Humpty Here—less of the nasturtiums. I might be wearing yellow clothing, but there's nothing of the coward about me. Just let old Monstro show his ugly face in this city and I'll show you what I can do. One little wish and that'll be the end of him.

King (*thoughtfully*) Hmmm. In that case, I suppose we'd better let you go. But don't think you're going to live in the lap of luxury and do nothing. We'll find you something useful to do.

Humpty Oh, I don't know about that, Mr King. You see, I haven't got a proper brain.

King Very well. We'll make you a shop steward. Report to the palace in half an hour. (*To the crowd*) Off you go, everybody. The excitement's over.

The crowd exits followed by the King and Powder and Shott

Mary (*delightedly*) Oh, Humpty. We're *so* pleased for you.

Polly Now you'll be able to make *lots* of friends.

Tommy And if the Sorcerer or his henchman turn up, there'll be a big surprise in store for them.

Jack Yes. From now on neither us, or our neighbours, have a thing to worry about.

Humpty (*puzzled*) What's a neighbour?

Dame What's a neighbour? *I'll* tell you what a neighbour is. A neighbour's a person who *borrows things.*

Mary (*laughing*) Really, Dame Dobb. Don't you think you're being a bit *too* terse?

Dame (*puzzled*) Terse? What does *that* mean?

Humpty Oh I can tell you *that*. Whenever they have a funeral in Yorkshire, t'hearse goes in the front.

Dame (*rolling her eyes*) Get into the palace. I'll make you all a nice cup of tea.

All exit amused

Grimm enters from the garden, leering

Grimm So—plotting against my master, eh? How lucky I happened to overhear. (*He sneers*) The fools. Don't they realize that no power on earth is greater than his. One wave of his hand, and it'll be the end of them all.

Mother Goose enters

Mother Goose (*as she comes in*)
Don't count your chickens before they're hatched;
We'll scotch your little game.
An end we'll bring to Monstro's plan,
Or Mother Goose is not my name.

Grimm Bah. You mealy mouthed old has-been. Not even you can stop my master now.

Mother Goose (*laughing*)
I wouldn't even waste my time.
Within the next few hours
The Sorcerer, if all goes well,
Will feel the force of Humpty's powers.
Then Nurs'ry-rhyme Land, by my troth,
Shall see the back of villains both.
(*She prods him with her spoon*)
So plot and plan, if that's your wish,
And on your master call;
But don't forget these parting words . . .
"Pride goes before a fall".

She exits

Grimm (*glaring after her*) How right you are, madam. How right you are.

(*To the audience*) But now to finish the task I began earlier. To find a bride for my mighty master. (*He leers*) I think Mistress Mary would be the *perfect* choice—don't you?

He laughs triumphantly and exits

Black-out

SCENE 4

A Corridor in the King's Palace

The Lights come up full

Powder and Shott enter looking disgruntled

Powder Huh. Fancy being made redundant by an *egg*.

Shott Well, what did you expect? Who needs an army when they've got somebody who's only to *wish* to make things turn out right? Some people have all the luck.

Powder Blooming Humpty Dumpty. If it wasn't for *him*, we'd still be in work.

Shott (*shrugging*) Oh, well. I suppose we can find something else to do for a living, but knowing *our* luck, it'll be something horrible like digging ditches.

Powder What's horrible about that?

Shott (*surprised*) It's hard work, digging ditches. I'm not so sure I'm well enough to do hard labour.

Powder Course you are. Don't you remember the last time you were up in court? The judge *said* you were.

Shott Yes. But I'm delicate, I am. I come from a very refined family. In fact *my* family tree goes right back to the time we *lived* in it.

Powder (*disbelievingly*) Give over. You'll be telling me next that they were all in the Ark with Noah.

Shott (*pityingly*) Don't be so stupid. Of course they weren't. They had their *own* boat.

Powder Huh. Well you're not the only one whose family goes back a long time. My family came over here with the Romans.

Shott Yes. But the immigration laws weren't as strict as they are today. (*He chortles*)

Powder (*stung*) Here . . . are you trying to incinerate that you're superior to me, or something?

Shott Well *of course* I'm superior to you. Look at you. The only man in the country who's been sent to jail for making big money.

Powder (*defensively*) It was only a *quarter of an inch* too big.

Shott Let's face it. You're absolutely stupid, you are. Nothing but a first class fool.

Powder Oh, you can sneer. But I'm not as big a fool as I used to be.

Shott Why? Have you been on a diet?

Powder No, but I spent most of this morning in the palace library reading some of the King's books.

Shott (*interested*) Eh? What sort of books has he got?
Powder Oh, all sorts. He's got *one* book that tells you about all the signs of the zodiac.
Shott (*scornfully*) Signs of the zodiac. What's so special about them? Everybody knows what *they* are.
Powder All right then, genius. What are they?
Shott (*thinking furiously*) Er—er . . .
Powder (*gloating*) Come on. Come on. (*He recites*) Leo, the Lion . . . Taurus, the Bull . . . Cancer, the Crab.
Shott *Bugs, the Bunny?*

Powder chortles with glee

(*Put out*) Well—anybody can make a mistake. There's no need to go into hysterics. I might not know much about zodiac signs, but I bet I know more about financial matters than you do. (*Smugly*) I've got a good head for money, I have.
Powder Yes. There's a little slot, just where your parting ought to be. (*He laughs*) All right then. Try this. Multiply five hundred and sixty pounds by six hundred and fifty pounds.
Shott I can't do *that*.
Powder *I* can. It's three hundred and sixty-four thousand pounds. (*He preens himself*)
Shott Well . . . (*He moves away*) I'm not surprised *you* managed it so fast.
Powder Why not?
Shott Everybody knows fools multiply rapidly these days.

Shott exits quickly. Powder reacts then races off after him

Humpty enters at the opposite side

Humpty Hiya, kids. (*He beams*) Cor, isn't it smashing living in a palace? I haven't stopped eating and drinking since I got here. That Dame Dobb —every few minutes she's bringing me cups of tea. I've had twenty-seven cups in the last half-hour. She says it's to keep me going—and it *does*. But I'm not going to tell you *where*.

Babes enter in party dresses

Hello . . . it's all the little palace children. What are you doing here?
Babe We wanted to meet you, Mr Dumpty.
Humpty Isn't that nice? They wanted to meet me. (*To the Babes*) Well, here I am, and we're going to have lots of fun together, aren't we? Anything you want . . . all you have to do is to let me know and I'll be able to wish for it straight away. But first I'm going to make a special wish of my own. I'm going to wish that you, and all the people out there in the audience, will join in a special song so we can get to know each other a little bit better. Shall I do that? (*He closes his eyes to wish*)

There is a flash and music begins

SONG *4*

At the end of the song, Humpty and the Babes exit happily

The Lights fade to Black-out

SCENE 5

The Great Ballroom of the Palace

A great ballroom with a staircase, pillars and arches. The King's throne is R of the staircase

King Florimund is seated on his throne in splendid robes. A Page stands at his side. Courtiers, etc., crowd the ballroom, and a stately dance performed by characters in Nursery-rhyme Land's national costume is in progress. At the end of the dance, the onlookers, including Polly and Jack, applaud politely and the dancers fall back into pre-arranged positions. King Florimund rises and moves down C

King Beautiful, beautiful. Absolutely beautiful. The national costumes are still as attractive as ever—(*he coughs*)—and as dusty. (*He clears his throat*) Loyal subjects of Nursery-rhyme Land, welcome to my royal palace and official birthday party.

All react with pleasure

In accordance with tradition, before the feasting begins, I intend to grant the first three requests placed before me, and *this* year—to make it even *more* exciting—no matter *what* the requests are, they'll be granted at once by my personal wisher—Humpty Dumpty.

There is a buzz of excitement

Are the suppliants in waiting?
Page Outside the ballroom, Your Majesty.
King Very well then. (*He moves back to the throne*) Announce them at once. (*He sits*)
Page (*unrolling his scroll*) Little Bo-peep.

Bo-peep enters and curtsies to the King

Bo-peep If it please Your Majesty, I've lost my sheep *again* and I don't know *where* to find them. Do you think Humpty Dumpty can help me?
King No trouble at all, my dear. The moment he arrives, you'll have them back in their pens.

Bo-peep withdraws to join the crowd

Page Dame Dobb, the royal housekeeper.

Dame Dobb enters in a fantastic gown

The onlookers react and King Florimund rises

King (*startled*) Halitosis, my dear. Don't tell me *you've* got a request?
Dame I certainly have. I want permission to get married.

All react in surprise

King Married? But—but—you *can't*. I mean . . . I haven't even proposed to you, yet.
Dame Oh, I'm not marrying you, Florimund. I'm marrying a magician.
King *Magician?*
Dame Yes. He took me out in his car this afternoon and turned it into a lovers' lane. (*She simpers*)
King (*dazed*) But what about *me*? Oh, I know I've fought against it, but surely you know how *I* feel about you? You're my cloud with a silver lining . . . the sunshine of my life . . . my breath of fresh air. You're the only woman who's ever reigned in my heart.
Dame Blimey. Is that a proposal or a weather forecast? (*Firmly*) No, Florimund, I'm sorry. You've left it too late. I want to marry Humpty.
King (*astounded*) *What?* That addle-pated, obsolescent *ovoid*? I won't allow it. (*Very firmly*) Permission *refused*.

All react in shock

Dame (*startled*) *Refused?* But you *can't* refuse. It's the . . .
King (*cutting her off*) Silence. Or I'll have you banished from the kingdom.

Everyone reacts. Dame Dobb reels and is quickly supported by Polly and Jack

Announce the next suppliant. (*He sits down in a temper*)
Page Tommy Tittlemouse and Mary Quite Contrary.

Tommy and Mary enter hand in hand

Mary (*happily*) Hello, Uncle Florimund.
Tommy Your Majesty.

They defer to King Florimund who rises in amazement

King Mary. What on earth do *you* want?
Mary (*beaming*) We want to get married.
King (*exploding*) Married? Nonsense. (*He stamps his bad foot*) Owwwww.

Everyone reacts

Permission refused. You can't possibly marry a *commoner*. I've got *far* better plans in mind for *you*.

Grimm enters at the top of the stairs

Grimm And so have *I*.

He moves down C, all edging away as he does so

Dame Oh—it's *him*. Tonsilitis.
King *Tonsilitis?*
Dame Yes. The original pain in the neck.

Grimm (*snarling*) Silence, you old hag, or I'll carve you into little pieces and feed you to the crows.

King (*recovering himself*) W—who are you? How *dare* you burst in here.

Grimm (*turning to him*) Who am I? I am Grimm, henchman to Monstro the Sorcerer—new ruler of this miserable little kingdom.

All react

King (*nervously*) W—w—what do you want?

Grimm A bride for my master . . .

Dame (*with great drama*) No. I won't go. I won't. (*She clutches at Jack*)

Grimm (*ignoring her*) And *she*—(*indicating Mary*)—is the one I choose.

Big reaction from all

Mary No. (*She clings to Tommy*)

Tommy Don't worry, Mary. He won't lay a finger on you. (*He moves to Grimm*) Clear off, you ugly looking brute, before I punch you on the nose.

Grimm (*amused*) You? (*He laughs*) Why, you miserable little pipsqueak. I've eaten bigger than you for breakfast. Out of my way.

He sweeps Tommy aside with a blow. Tommy crashes to the floor and all gasp with fear. Mary hurries to him, but is grabbed by Grimm

Mary (*struggling*) Let go of me. Let go. Help.

King (*anguished*) Somebody *do* something. (*To Powder and Shott*) Stop him.

Powder (*shaking his head*) Not us. You've given us the sack.

King (*pleading*) I'll give anything to the one who saves her.

Humpty appears on the stairs

Humpty Don't worry, folks. *I'll* save her. (*To Grimm*) Hey—frogspawn features.

Grimm (*turning, but still holding Mary*) Whaaaaaaat?

Humpty (*coming down the stairs*) Let go of my friend.

Grimm (*with a cruel grin*) Why don't you try and *make* me? (*He turns away again*)

Humpty All right. I will. (*He kicks Grimm up the backside*)

Grimm Owwwwww. (*He releases Mary and spins to face Humpty*) Why, you little worm. I'll break every bone in your body. (*He advances on Humpty*)

Humpty (*retreating*) Ooo-er . . . (*He steps back and cannons into the King*)

Grimm (*grabbing him*) Now then . . . (*He begins to shake him*)

Humpty (*anguished*) Oh, I wish you'd buzz off back to where you came from.

There is a flash and Grimm begins buzzing loudly. All watch with amusement

He scuttles up the stairs and exits rapidly

Dame He's gone.

Mary (*running to Humpty*) Oh, Humpty. You were *marvellous*. (*She hugs him tightly*)

King (*grabbing his hand and pumping it vigorously*) My dear boy. I don't know how to thank you. You saved us all. Name your own reward. Anything you want you can have.

Humpty (*grimacing*) Can I have my hand back?

The King quickly lets go of his hand

Oooooh. You aren't half strong. (*Eagerly*) Here, do you really mean that? I can have anything at all?

King (*agreeing*) Absolutely anything.

Humpty Well . . . how about a wedding, then?

King Wedding? Wedding? You shall have a bigger wedding than Charles and Lady Di had in nineteen eighty-one.

Dame (*overcome*) Oh, Humpty. Married at long last.

King And I know Dame Dobb will make you a wonderful wife.

Dame Oh, I will. I will.

Humpty Eh? (*He realizes*) Oh, it's not her I'm going to marry. It's Mary.

All react

Tommy (*anxiously*) But Humpty—Mary's going to marry *me*.

Humpty No she isn't. (*He indicates the King*) He said he wouldn't let her—I heard him. So that means she's free to marry *me*.

Mary (*kindly*) But Humpty, I'm not in *love* with you.

Humpty Pooh. What does that matter? I can soon change that with one of my wishes. (*Excitedly*) Oooh, Mary. I can have you all to myself now. Me and you—forever.

Mary (*dismayed*) Humpty. That's *very* selfish.

Humpty (*drunk with power*) I don't care. I don't care. I've just realized I can have anything I want. Anything in the whole wide world, *and nobody can stop me*.

King (*fuming*) We'll see about that. I'm still the King around here and you'll do as I tell you to.

Humpty (*rudely*) Rubbish. One snap of my fingers and I can blow this whole kingdom to bits.

Everyone moves back quickly

King (*to Powder and Shott*) You two. I'm giving you your old jobs back. Arrest him at once.

Humpty (*warningly*) Keep back. Take one step and I'll do something desperate.

No-one moves

Dame (*impatiently*) Well don't just stand there. He's only bluffing. He wouldn't *really* do it. Grab him.

Everyone creeps menacingly towards Humpty who retreats right down c

Humpty Keep back. I'm warning you. I'll do it. I *will*. All right, then . . .

(*Loudly*) I wish this entire kingdom would collapse like a pack of cards.

There is a flash and a loud crack of thunder. The Lights flicker. Everyone freezes for a second, then absolute chaos breaks out. Everyone screams and staggers back. There is a terrible crash and a Black-out. In the darkness, the lane cloth comes in behind Humpty and the screams and noises die away to absolute silence

Everyone, except Humpty, exits

SCENE 6

The Ruins of Nursery-rhyme Land

A desolate plain strewn with ruined buildings, or a simple black lane cloth

Humpty's voice is heard in the Black-out

Humpty (*uncertainly*) Ha har . . . that showed you, didn't it? That scared you. Didn't think I could do it, eh? Now who's boss? (*Silence*) Well . . . if you'll all promise to behave yourselves and do what I want you to, I'll put everything back together again. All right? (*Absolute silence*) It— it won't take me a couple of seconds. (*Silence*) All right, then . . . if you promise. I wish everything were back to normal again.

Nothing happens

Er—I said, "I wish everything were back to normal again." (*Again, nothing happens*) Come on. Let's have some light and things. I've wished. (*Silence*) Is anybody there? Hello? Alec? Alectrician? (*More timidly*) Hello?

Very very slowly the darkness around him lifts until he is visible. He is sitting c, curled up into a tight ball with only his face visible. He is alone

(*Looking around*) Oh, no. (*Unbelievingly*) The magic—it's gone. I've got no wishes left. What have I *done*?

Mother Goose enters slowly. A misty spotlight picks her out

Mother Goose (*softly*) Yes, Humpty. What *have* you done?
Humpty (*jumping up*) Oh, Mother Goose, thank goodness you've come. (*Almost in tears*) I've destroyed all of Nursery-rhyme Land and lost my magic powers. You've got to help me put things right again—*please*.
Mother Goose (*shaking her head sadly*) I'm sorry, Humpty. Not even *my* magic is strong enough to do that. You were the only one who had so much power. (*Gently*) You *were* warned about using it selfishly.
Humpty (*fighting back tears*) I'm sorry. I didn't mean to do it. I just got too big for my boots and wanted my own way. I didn't realize I could cause so much damage. I wanted to teach them all a lesson . . . but it's *me* who's been taught, isn't it? (*Breaking down*) The only trouble is, now I've learnt it, it's too late to do any good.

He buries his face in his hands and sobs, sinking to his knees before Mother Goose. For a moment she looks down gently and observes him, then firms her shoulders

Mother Goose (*firmly*) Regrets? Mistakes? What's done is done;
> One has to look ahead.
> Come on, young Humpty. Dry your eyes.
> Stop wishing you were dead.

There is the clear "ping" of a triangle, and she looks up in surprise

> Well, bless my soul. What have we here? (*She extends her hand*)
> A tiny, whirling flake
> Of glist'ning, frosty, pure white snow. (*She inspects it*)
> It is. There's no mistake.
> Beneath a blanket soft and deep—
> (Within the hour, I fear)
> These silent ruins soon will sleep.
> So come. You can't stay here.

She assists him to rise

> You'll need a place to rest your head—
> Some shelter from the skies—
> Whilst a world of snow and fantasy
> Appears before your eyes.

She waves her spoon and the lane cloth opens to reveal:

~~SCENE~~ Song 5,

A World of Ice and Snow

A glittering, fantastic snow setting. If possible, a snow wheel should be projected over the whole set so that falling flakes are visible throughout the scene. The Lights are cold white and ice-blue shadow

Choristers and Babes perform a ballet of winter, slow and graceful

Mother Goose exits silently with Humpty as the ballet commences

At the end of the ballet all adopt a graceful pose

Mother Goose, in a glittering cloak, enters up C *and moves downstage*

Mother Goose Around this spot where laughter rang,
> The North Wind coldly sighs;
> But fear you not—for come the spring—
> Once more shall Nursery Land arise.

A brief coda to the ballet is performed, and transforms itself into a tableaux as—

the CURTAIN *falls*

ACT II

Scene 1

Dame Dobb's Farm in Story-book Land ·

The farmyard setting depicts an old barn and views of ploughed land in the background. There is a haywain L and haystacks etc R. It is a fine spring morning and everything looks pleasant

Tommy, Mary, Jack and Polly, all dressed in shabby but clean clothes, lead the Choristers in a bright and cheery song

SONG 7

At the end of the song the Choristers move back into predetermined positions and chatter quietly amongst themselves

Mary Oh, I can hardly believe it. The first day of spring and a marvellous new country to live in.

Tommy Thank goodness we managed to make our way here after Nursery-rhyme Land collapsed.

Polly Yes. We certainly couldn't have wished for a better spot. Dame Dobb certainly knew what she was doing when she bought this place.

Jack I'll say. Living on a farm seems to agree with all of us, even though it *has* been hard work these last few months.

Mary (*wistfully*) Of course, it'll never be the same as our *real* home.

Polly But at least we're *safe*—and miles away from Monstro and that horrible henchman of his. They'll never find us here.

Jack That's true. If they *were* going to, they'd have done it long ago. It's been months since the night of the Ball.

Mary (*covering her ears*) Oh, please, I don't want to hear another word about that dreadful night. From now on we've got to do our best to forget all that happened and try to make a new life for ourselves here in Story-book Land.

Tommy Mary's right. There's still lots to do before we get the place in *real* running order. How on earth we've managed so far, I can't imagine. There are so many mouths to feed. (*Briskly*) Now then, has anyone seen the King lately?

Choristers gather round

Polly Well the last time *I* saw him, he was driving a steam roller all over the potato fields.

Mary Whatever for?

Polly He *said* he was trying to grow *mashed* potatoes.

Tommy (*laughing*) Poor King Florimund. I'm afraid he'll never make a real farmer.

Jack I know. He fell off the barn *roof* this morning.

Mary (*concerned*) Oh. He didn't hurt himself, did he?

Jack Oh, no. *Fortunately* there was a haystack below to break his fall.

All smile with relief

Unfortunately though, a pitchfork was sticking up in it.

All gasp

Fortunately he missed it.

All sigh with relief

But *un*fortunately, he missed the *haystack* too. (*He grins*) Still . . . he seemed to be enjoying himself, and that's all that matters, isn't it?

Tommy Well, we'd better be getting back to work, I suppose. Come on, everyone. The tea break's over.

With mock groans, Polly, Jack and the Choristers exit cheerfully

I'd better make a start on those broken fences . . . (*He begins to exit*)

Mary (*quickly*) Oh, Tommy . . .

Tommy (*turning to her*) Yes?

Mary (*hesitantly*) Promise you won't be cross if I tell you a secret.

Tommy (*laughing*) Why should I be? What is it?

Mary *I* know where Humpty is.

Tommy (*annoyed*) *Humpty? That* spiteful, bad-tempered little monster.

Mary (*quickly*) But he's not, Tommy. That was all a mistake. He told me so. He couldn't *help* himself.

Tommy (*grimly*) I'll give him "mistake". Destroying our lovely little country like that. Where is he?

Mary (*firmly*) I'm not going to tell you if you're going to be nasty to him. But just in case you're interested, if it hadn't been for *him*, we'd all have *starved* to death before today.

Tommy (*startled*) Pardon?

Mary (*turning away*) Where do you think the food's been coming from that Dame Dobb cooks? *We* hadn't the money to pay for it.

Tommy You're not telling me that Humpty's been providing it?

Mary He certainly *has*. (*She turns to him*) He's been working day and night all over the countryside to earn enough money to keep us going till our own crops grow.

Tommy But—but where's he been hiding himself?

Mary Here on the farm. Dame Dobb and I have been taking care of him. We didn't tell you before because we knew both you *and* Uncle Florimund were still cross with him, but now—as it *is* Spring—well . . . don't you think it's time to let bygones be bygones?

Tommy Oh, well . . . I suppose it's no use holding grudges forever—and if what you say is true, he certainly seems to be trying to make up for

what he did. All right. I'll shake hands with him . . . but before we do anything else, we'd better go and break the news to His Majesty.

Mary (*hugging him*) I was hoping you'd say that. Come on. Let's go tell him now.

Mary takes his hand and leads him off

Grimm appears from behind the haystack, triumphantly smiling

Grimm At last. For six long months I have searched for their hiding place, and now—I've found it. (*He laughs*) Oh, mighty master, your bride will soon be with you. Within the hour, Mistress Mary will be in my hands and on her way to your enchanted castle. But first, I must find some helpers. No screaming female is going to get her little claws near *my* pretty face. (*He leers, then glances off*) Someone's coming.

He quickly exits behind the haystack

A moment

Powder and Shott enter. They are in very ragged clothes and are quite annoyed

Powder Oh, I'm fed up of this, I am. I've never had to work so hard in all my life.

Shott Me neither. Every time I try to milk that funny coloured cow over there (*he indicates*) it chases me all round the field.

Powder Which funny coloured cow? (*He looks*) Fool. That's not funny coloured. It's a *Jersey*.

Shott Oh. I thought it was its *skin*.

Powder (*wincing*) Oooh, you get worse, you do. (*Impatiently*) Now hurry up and collect that horse. I want to get back to the farmhouse and have something to eat.

Shott (*blankly*) Horse? What horse?

Powder What do you mean, "what horse"? The King's *favourite* horse. The one he told you to take out this morning and have shod.

Shott (*startled*) Oh, blimey. I thought he said, "Take it out and have it *shot*." I've just got back from burying it.

Powder (*horrified*) Oh, no.

Grimm emerges from behind the haystack

Grimm Ahaaaaaa.

Shott (*distraught*) Oh, go away. We haven't time to be bothered with you. We're in terrible trouble.

Powder The King's going to go crackers when he finds out what's happened.

Grimm Indeed? (*He leers*) But what if he *doesn't* find out? What then?

Shott (*almost in tears*) Of course he's going to find out. He can't help it. I've just shot his favourite horse.

Grimm (*beaming*) Then why not let *me* replace it?

Powder Don't be daft. He'd spot the difference right away. He'd never fit a saddle on *you*.

Grimm (*giving a pained look*) I mean why not let me *buy* another horse for the old fool?

They both look interested

That way, no-one need ever know but you and me. (*He leers*).

Shott Do you mean it? Honest?

Grimm Of course, but I'd expect a little *help* in return, you understand?

Powder What sort of help?

Grimm (*lowering his voice*) One of my master's slaves—a certain *female*—has run away from his enchanted castle. Help me to recapture her, and this money—(*he produces a bag of coins*)—is yours.

Shott (*uncertain*) Well . . .

Grimm (*dangling the bag*) It's the answer to your problem.

Powder (*snatching the bag*) We'll do it. Where is she?

Grimm (*smiling in triumph*) I knew you'd see sense. Follow me. She'll be along in a moment.

Grimm gives a bellowing laugh and exits in a swirl. Powder and Shott follow him nervously

Dame (*off, calling*) Yoo-hoo. Humpty?

She enters clutching a covered basket, and wearing an outrageous costume of rustic origin

Yoo-hoo? (*She looks round then moves down* C) That's funny. He should have been here by now. (*She shrugs*) Oh, well. I suppose he'll be along soon. (*She puts the basket down*) Oh, boys and girls. What a time we're having down here on the farm. There's all sorts of exciting things going on. Last week we had some sheep-dog trials—and they were all found not guilty. Then King Florimund managed to cross a hen with a banjo, and came up with a chicken that could pluck itself. And the poor old Crooked Man—remember him? Well he'd just climbed over the crooked style when the Cow With the Crumpled Horn came up behind him and gave him a terrible kick. (*She winces*) Oooh. I'm not saying *where* it kicked him, but if his head had been in Scotland, and his feet had been in London, he'd have had a terrible pain in the Midlands. Mind you, it hasn't all been fun. We'd only been here two days when I fell down the bedroom stairs and broke my leg. I had it in plaster right up to here. (*She indicates*) The doctor was furious. "Dame Dobb," he said, "you mustn't go *near* those stairs again until I take this plaster-cast off." Oh, it *was* a relief when he did. You've no idea how difficult it is climbing up a drainpipe to get to bed.

Humpty and several Girls enter pulling a rope that is obviously tied to something off-stage

Humpty (*brightly*) Hiya, kids. Hello, Dame Dobb.

Dame (*moving up to him*) Never mind, "Hello, Dame Dobb". What have you got there?

Humpty A surprise.

Dame Surprise? What sort of surprise?
Humpty Well . . . just give us a hand to pull it on, and you'll see.

Dame Dobb grabs hold of the rope and all heave at it. With much puffing and panting, they back across the farmyard

> *Humpty finally vanishes from sight into the wings and dashes round the back of the set unseen*

Dame Dobb and the Girls continue pulling

> *Humpty, a big grin on his face, enters at the other end of the rope*

Dame Dobb reacts and flings the rope down

> *The Girls laugh merrily and exit with the rope*

Dame (*put out*) I might have expurgated something like that from you. Come over here and get your dinner. (*She goes back to her basket*)
Humpty (*eagerly*) Oooh, what is it?
Dame It's a nice big bowl of gold soup. (*She picks up the basket*)
Humpty *Gold soup?*
Dame Yes. I made it with fourteen carrots.
Humpty Oh. I'm not very fond of carrots, Dame Dobb. Haven't you got anything else?
Dame (*producing a small pie*) Well . . . there's this meat pie. (*She hands it to him*)
Humpty Oh, I like these. (*He takes a bite*) Ughhhhhh. It's terrible.
Dame That just shows how little *you* know about food. The recipe book distinctly says that those pies are delicious.
Humpty Oh . . . well, I don't think I'll bother with anything to eat, if you don't mind. As a matter of fact, I'm going to watch the football match and I don't want to be late.
Dame (*interested*) Oh—I like a nice game of football myself. Which team do you support?
Humpty (*Names local team*)
Dame That's nice. And do you get that twitchy, feverish tingle of excitement rushing over you when they win their matches?
Humpty I don't know. I've only been supporting them for two seasons. Oh, by the way, they're having a big charity match next week and all the tickets are free. I've got a spare one. Would you like to buy it?
Dame Well . . . how much is it?
Humpty Twenty pounds.
Dame (*aghast*) *Twenty pounds?* I could go into (*local district*) and get myself a man for that.
Humpty Yes. But you wouldn't get forty-five minutes each way and a brass band at half-time. (*He chortles*)

Dame Dobb turns away in disgust then reacts at something she sees off stage

Dame Ooooh.
Humpty (*startled*) What is it?

Dame (*pointing*) Look. Two little calves rubbing noses.
Humpty What about it?
Dame (*coyly*) Well . . . whenever I see *that* happening . . . it makes *me* want to do the same. (*She gives him a "come hither" look*)
Humpty Well what's stopping you? They're your animals.
Dame (*disgustedly*) Oh, I give up. It's useless trying to talk to you about romance. You're about as passionate as a bowl of cold porridge.
Humpty No I'm not. I'm very passionate, I am—and especially when I've got a heavy cold.
Dame (*curious*) What's having a heavy cold got to do with it?
Humpty Well, every time I sneeze, I get this uncontrollable urge to kiss a pretty girl.
Dame (*startled*) Good heavens. And what are you taking for it?
Humpty Snuff.

They sing

SONG 8

As the song ends, King Florimund enters in a temper, followed by Tommy, Mary, Polly, Jack and the Choristers

King (*triumphantly*) Aha . . . Caught you red handed. (*He advances on Humpty*)
Mary (*anxiously*) Uncle Florimund, please . . .
King (*to Humpty*) How *dare* you follow us to our secret hide-away, you snake in wolf's clothing. Haven't you done enough damage? Clear off before I have you thrown into the nearest duck-pond.
Tommy Your Majesty, wait. Don't you think you're being a little *too* hard on him. After all, he *has* tried to make up for what he did.
Dame Yes, he has.
King (*whirling round to face Tommy*) It's all right for *you* Tommy Tittle-mouse. You haven't had *your* kingdom blown to pieces by this ob-streperous ovoid. When he came out of that egg, he was supposed to help us defeat the Sorcerer, wasn't he?
Polly Yes, Your Majesty—but he had magic powers, then.
King And whose fault was it that he lost them? His *own*. (*He faces Humpty again*) Well if you want to be forgiven, you can go and do the job you were sent to do—and don't come back until you've done it. (*He stamps his foot firmly, and yells in pain*)
Jack Your Majesty. You can't send him off to the Sorcerer's castle alone.
Dame It's a terrible place, according to the stories we've heard.
Polly Everyone who enters it goes *mad*.
Humpty Blimey. It sounds like the Council Offices at (*local town*). (*Bravely*) Oh, well . . . if you've gotta go, you've gotta go. Which way is it?
King *I* don't know. That's *your* problem. But don't forget. If you don't get rid of Monstro, then you needn't come back here. Understand?

The King stamps off in high dudgeon

Humpty (*unhappily*) Well . . . cheerio, kids. (*He edges his way to an exit*)

Mary (*hurrying to him*) Oh, Humpty. Take care. (*She hugs him*)
Humpty Bye-bye, Mary.

He exits dejectedly

Dame (*sobbing*) Oh, poor Humpty. Just as he's realized he can't live
without me, he's going to have to.
Polly He doesn't stand a chance, poor thing.
Tommy Don't worry, folks. Jack and I are going after him—but not a
word to the King. With three of us to fight him, old Monstro won't
stand a chance.
Jack Quick. Back to the farmhouse and get the swords.

*Jack, Tommy, Dame Dobb and the Choristers bustle off with much
excitement*

Mary (*worriedly*) Oh, Polly. If only there was something *we* could do.
Polly Cheer up, Mary. If it *is* possible to put an end to Monstro, Tommy
and Jack are the ones to do it.

Grimm enters stealthily behind them

After all, they're the bravest boys in the whole wide world.

Grimm signals off

*Powder and Shott enter holding two opened blankets. These are held so
that neither of the men can see the girls*

Mary But all the same . . .

Grimm swiftly steps to the front of the girls

Ohhhhhhh.
Grimm (*loudly*) Now.

*Powder and Shott fling the blankets over the girls' heads, and toss the girls
over their shoulders. As the girls struggle and kick, Grimm laughs in triumph*

To the castle of the Sorcerer.

All exit

Black-out

SCENE 2

A Path in the Great Forest

The Lights come up to give a gloomy effect

Mother Goose enters

Mother Goose I was wondering just how long it would take before Grimm
showed his ugly face again. Poor Polly and Mary . . . carried off to live
in Monstro's castle for the rest of their lives. Not that *that's* going to be
very long from what *I* know about him. He's got a nasty habit of
getting bored with wives and servants, and either turns them into

animals for hunting, or little china dancing dolls. (*Brightening*) Still, not
to worry. Humpty, Tommy and Jack are all in hot pursuit of him, and
with a little bit of help from *me*, stand a very good chance of putting him
firmly in his place—not to mention rescuing their sweethearts. But first
of all, I'd better make sure they all come in this direction. We don't
want them getting lost in the Great Forest, do we? Now here's where
you can all help. When I wave my magic spoon, I want you all to shout
out as loud as you can, this special magic spell: *Bibbidi Bobbidi Boo*.
Will you do that for me? Right. One magic spell coming up.

*She waves her spoon and calls with the audience. The Lights flicker then
return to original setting. She glances off*

And here they come.

Humpty enters singing. He carries a cudgel

Humpty When you walk through a storm, hold your head up high . . .
Hiya, kids. (*He sees Mother Goose*) Oooh. It's Mother Duck, again.
Hello. What are *you* doing here?
Mother Goose Oh, just what I'm normally doing, Humpty. Trying to keep
an eye on things.
Humpty Well thank goodness I've met you, 'cos I seem to have got lost.
I'm looking for the Sorcerer's castle, but I can't find it anywhere.
Mother Goose (*amused*) Never mind, Humpty. As soon as Tommy and
Jack arrive, I'll put you on the right track.
Humpty Tommy and Jack?
Mother Goose (*nodding*) You didn't think they'd let you go off to fight old
Monstro, alone, did you? No. They've been following your footsteps
for miles, ready to defend you if anything went wrong. In fact, here
they are now.

Tommy and Jack enter, swords drawn

Tommy (*surprised*) Mother Goose.
Mother Goose (*smiling*) Well don't look so surprised. I'm still your fairy
godmother, despite what's happened to Nursery-rhyme Land. Now
come over here. We've got some serious talking to do if you're going to
reach Monstro's castle in time.
Jack In time for what?
Mother Goose (*annoyed with herself*) Tch, tch. There I go again. For-
getting you don't know what happened whilst you were searching for
your swords.
Tommy What was it?
Mother Goose Grimm arrived and kidnapped both Mary *and* Polly.
Tommy⎫
Jack ⎬(*together*) Oh, no.
Humpty⎭
Mother Goose (*nodding*) I'm afraid so. They'll be arriving at the castle *any
time now*, and unless we can move quickly, come the morning, they'll
be done for.

Tommy (*urgently*) We've got to save them. Oh, please . . . How do we get there? Which way do we go?

Mother Goose You haven't a hope of finding your way without a guide. The enchanted castle lies beside a great lake in the middle of the forest. No-one has ever set eyes on it and lived to tell the tale.

Tommy (*remembering*) But *I* have. On the morning that Humpty fell off the wall. I was fishing in the lake. (*To Jack*) Don't you remember?

Jack (*excitedly*) Of course. The trout for King Florimund.

Tommy I could find my way there blindfolded. (*To the others*) Come on.

Mother Goose Wait. The secret of Monstro's power is the great jewel he wears in his turban. Get your hands on that and he'll be helpless.

Humpty Don't you worry, Mother Duck. That jewel will be ours before (*Trade Union leader*) can call another strike.

Mother Goose So be it. (*She raises her wooden spoon*) To the Sorcerer's castle. But before we go, a magic spell to keep you safe from harm. (*To the audience*) Come on, children. Same magic words as before: Bibbidi . . . Bobbidi . . . Boo.

They sing

SONG 9

They all exit cheerily as the song ends

Black-out

SCENE 3

Outside Monstro's Castle

A grim, gothic-style castle, with moss-covered walls, which stands on the edge of a lake. There is a huge door C of the wall and at each side are burning torches. Trees with almost human faces flank the castle down L and R

The Lights come up to give a blue, green and red effect on a group of Hungarian Gypsies who are performing a lively csárdás with much banging of tambourines and shouts

Grimm enters L as the dance ends, followed by Powder and Shott who still carry the now silent girls

Grimm (*gnashing his teeth at the Gypsies*) Away with you, you filthy vermin.

The Gypsies depart with much glowering

Grimm signals to Powder and Shott

Into the castle with them.

Powder and Shott move into the castle through the door C, and, after giving a quick look about him, Grimm follows. The door closes

Tommy, Jack and Humpty enter cautiously R, weapons at the ready

Humpty (*cheerily*) Hiya, kids. (*He sees the castle and sings*) Camelot . . . Camelot . . .

Jack ⎱
Tommy ⎰ (*together; anguished*) Shhhhhhhh!

Humpty (*lowering his voice*) Cor . . . what a creepy-looking place. It looks just like a Butlin's holiday camp in the off-season.

Tommy Well, it certainly doesn't look very inviting, but never mind that. How are we going to get inside?

Jack Yes. By the look of that door, it'll be almost impossible.

Humpty No it won't. I've got an idea.

Tommy What is it?

Humpty Watch this. (*Before anyone can stop him, he hammers loudly on the door with his cudgel*) Knock, knock.

As Tommy and Jack react in horror, a loud voice is heard. This is best done on an off-stage microphone

Monstro (*off*) Who's there?

Humpty (*calling*) Wendy.

Monstro (*off*) Wendy who?

Humpty (*singing*) Wendy red, red, robin comes bob-bob-bobbing along . . . along. (*He jumps about in glee*)

There is a growl of annoyance from Monstro. Humpty hammers on the door again

Knock, knock.

Monstro (*off, snarling*) Who's there?

Humpty (*calling*) Hatch.

Monstro (*off*) Hatch who?

Humpty Bless you. (*Or gesundheit.*)

Monstro (*off, annoyed*) Who *is* that?

Humpty (*calling*) Dozen.

Monstro (*off, loudly*) Dozen who?

Humpty Dozen anybody want to come and let me in? (*He folds up with laughter*)

Monstro (*off, calling*) Grimm. Grimmmmmmmm. See who that is and tear off his head.

Humpty clutches at his neck in fright. Tommy and Jack quickly position themselves at either side of the door

A moment later the door flies open to reveal Grimm, sword in hand

Grimm (*seeing Humpty*) So.

Humpty (*singing*) A needle pulling thread . . . La, a note to follow soh . . .

Grimm charges out of the doorway and advances on Humpty

Tommy and Jack quickly enter the castle unseen

Grimm (*swaggering*) Well, well, well. If it isn't Mr Scrambled Egg, himself. (*He waves his sword under Humpty's nose*) And what might *you* be doing here? (*He rests the point of his sword at Humpty's throat*)

Humpty I've brought you a message from a well-wisher.

Grimm (*puzzled*) A well-wisher? What is it?

Humpty He wishes you were down a well. (*He giggles*)

Grimm (*annoyed*) Why, you miserable little cur. I'll have your head for that. (*He raises his sword*)

Humpty Wait. You can't.

Grimm Can't? *Can't? I* can do *anything.*

Humpty I bet *I* know something you can't do.

Grimm What is it?

Humpty I bet you can't milk chocolate.

Grimm (*livid*) Aaaaaaagh. I'm going to slice off your ears and throw them over there. (*He indicates*) Then I'll slice off your arms, and throw them over there. (*He indicates*) Slice off your legs and throw them over there. (*He indicates*) And finally—I'm going to slice off your head and throw it over there. (*He indicates*) Now what do you say to *that*?

Humpty I'll be fresh to the last slice.

Grimm gives a bellow of rage and raises his sword again

Humpty reacts, turns and runs for his life. Grimm chases after him and they exit

King Florimund and Dame Dobb enter wearily

Dame Ohhhh . . . Here we are at last.

King Thank goodness for that. I'm so tired, I can't walk another step.

Dame You can't be as tired as I am. I hardly slept a wink last night.

King Why not?

Dame Well . . . I accidently plugged my electric blanket into the toaster, and spent most of the night popping out of bed.

King (*looking around*) Are you sure this is the Sorcerer's castle, Halitosis?

Dame (*patiently*) Of course it's the Sorcerer's castle. Exactly where Mother Goose told us it would be. Now come on. Cheer up. I've never known anybody who could look as miserable as you can.

King It's all right for you. It's been a terrible day for me, this has. I was so depressed when I found out what had happened to Mary and Polly, I even tried to commit suicide.

Dame (*startled*) You *didn't.*

King (*nodding miserably*) I did. I bought a gallon of petrol, a box of matches, a bottle of poison, a long rope and a loaded revolver. Then I rowed a boat up the river, anchored it under a tree, tied the rope around a branch, put the other end round my neck, poured the petrol all over myself, set fire to it with the matches, swallowed the poison, put the revolver to my head and pulled the trigger.

Dame (*all agog*) And what happened?

King The bullet missed me, hit the rope and severed it, I fell out of the boat and into the river and that put the fire out. I swallowed so much water I brought up the poison, and if I hadn't been such a good swimmer, I could have *drowned.*

Dame (*to the audience*) And you think they have problems in (*TV soap opera*) Never mind, Florimund. Another few minutes and you won't

have a thing to worry about. The boys will have finished off old Monstro and we can all go back to Nursery-rhyme Land.

King Oh, I hope so. You've no idea how . . .

Humpty charges on and races past them before realizing they are there. He comes back, quickly

Humpty Ooooooh. Your Magneticals. Dame Dobb. What are you doing here?

King Waiting for you to rescue Mary and Polly. Where are they?

Humpty Still inside the castle. Tommy and Jack have gone looking for her, and I've pushed Grimm into the lake. Quick, we've got to get moving.

Dame (*firmly*) Now just a minute. I'm not moving anywhere. Not till I've had a chance to get my breath back. No matter what happens, I'm going to stay here for at least the next five minutes.

King Me too.

Humpty But you can't. Don't you realize where you are? This is the most dangerous place in the whole world.

Dame (*wide eyed*) You mean . . . (*names local district*)?

Humpty Even worse. This is the spot where the great Monster of the Lake comes to eat. Anybody found standing here, he'll eat without question.

King ⎱(*together*) Ooo-er.
Dame ⎰

Dame Whatever are we going to do?

Humpty There's only one thing we can do. We'll just have to sing as loudly as possible and try to frighten him away. And if he *does* come near perhaps all the children out there will warn us about him. (*To the audience*) Will you do that, kids?

Audience participation, then they begin to sing ~~SONG 10~~ *Song 8*

A weird Monster creeps on behind them after a couple of lines

As the audience react, the three play up to them

The King and Humpty finally see the Monster and dash into the castle

Dame Dobb continues singing alone. The Monster taps her on the shoulder. She turns to him and smiles

The Monster screams in terror and quickly exits

She turns back to the audience and shrugs

Black-out

SCENE 4

A Corridor inside the Castle

Powder and Shott enter, still carrying the two girls. With a sigh of relief, they lower the girls to their feet

Powder (*exhausted*) Ohhhhh. Thank goodness for that. I couldn't have carried her another inch.

Shott (*panting*) Me neither. I wonder who they are?

The two girls quickly throw off the blankets

Mistress Mary . . .

Powder And Polly Flinders.

Mary (*stamping her foot*) How *dare* you carry us off like this. Just wait till Uncle Florimund hears about it.

Polly Not to mention Jack and Tommy. They'll make you wish you'd never been born.

Powder (*alarmed*) Oo-er. It was all a mistake. We didn't know it was you.

Shott Old Grimm told us you were runaway slaves. Honest, he did.

Mary Slaves? *Slaves?* Do we *look* like slaves? (*To Polly*) Come on, Polly. We're going back to the farm right this instant.

Polly and Mary head for the exit

Grimm enters, dripping with weeds from the lake

As he does so, the girls walk straight into him

Grimm (*snarling*) Not so fast, my pretty ones. You're going *nowhere*.

The girls cower back

Take them to my master's den. (*He indicates off*)

Powder Do it yourself, you nasty-looking brute.

Shott Yes. We've finished giving *you* a hand. You're a double-crossing twister, you are. These are our friends.

Powder (*to the girls*) Don't worry, girls. He won't lay a finger on you.

Grimm (*savagely*) So—you dare to disobey me, do you? Very well, then. You shall suffer the consequences. (*He calls*) Guards. Guards.

Two menacing-looking Guards appear

Take these idiots to the dungeons and feed them to the rats.

The Guards grab Powder and Shott as Grimm turns to the girls

And as for you two, as soon as I've cleared away this slime, there's a pleasant little meeting with my master in store.

He gives a signal and the Guards force Powder and Shott off. With a sneer, Grimm exits opposite

Polly (*scared*) Oh, Mary. What are we going to do?

Mary (*bravely*) Don't be frightened, Polly. I'm sure someone will turn up to rescue us. (*She glances around*) What a horrible-looking place.

Polly (*glancing off*) Oh, look. (*She steps back in alarm*)

Mary What is it? Ooooh. (*She recoils*)

A stream of Mice pour on to the stage, surrounding them

As the girls cower together, the Mice perform a short menacing dance. It is suggested that the Babes be used for this routine

    Mother Goose appears R, *wooden spoon held aloft, as the dance ends*

    The Mice squeal in panic and exit quickly

Mother Goose.

The girls hurry to her in relief

Mother Goose (*beaming*) So this is where he's hiding you, is it? Hello, my dears. Sorry to have been so long, but we've just been making a few plans. Humpty, Tommy and Jack are all inside the castle and waiting for a chance to overthrow the Sorcerer. Don't be afraid. Just do your best to keep him occupied so he doesn't suspect what we're up to. All right?

Polly We'll try.

Mother Goose Now watch out. Grimm is on his way back to collect you, so I'd best be gone before he sees me. We've got to take him unawares.

    Mother Goose exits

    Grimm, who has cleaned himself up, enters

Grimm Right, my pretty ones. To Monstro's den.

    He grabs their arms and pulls them off stage

The Lights fade to Black-out

SCENE 5

Monstro's Den

This is a gothic hall with arched windows and great stone pillars. A great throne is up C *and up* L *is a large free-standing flat with two arched openings. Between these is a large wheel which can be turned in the manner of a ship's wheel. The flat is painted to depict a "transformation machine", and has as many vari-coloured lights and coiled cables as possible. Over each arch is a sign. One is marked "In", the other "Out". If it is not possible to have double two-way doors in the arches, back openings with black drapes*

The Lights come up on the empty hall

    Jack and Tommy, carrying swords, enter stealthily to creepy accompaniment from the orchestra

Tommy Well, this is the Sorcerer's den all right. But where's he?

Jack Who cares? Let's just find the girls and get out of here.

Tommy (*grimly*) Oh, no. Not now we've come *this* far. Unless we get rid of Monstro once and for all, we'll be looking over our shoulders for the rest of our lives.

Jack You're right, of course. But all the same, the sooner we get out of

this place the better. You can feel the evil all around. It's almost as if he's hiding somewhere, watching us.

Tommy Yes. We've got to keep out of his sight until one of us gets the chance to snatch that jewelled turban of his. You hide over there (*he points*) and the minute he comes in, I'll try to surprise him. Between us, we're going to give old Monstro the shock of his life.

Jack quickly exits

Right, Mr Sorcerer—(*he grasps his sword firmly*)—for once in your life you're not going to get everything your own way, because I'm about to start fighting for what's really *mine*. (*He sings*)

~~SONG 11~~

At the end of the song Monstro's voice is heard, off

Monstro (*off, calling*) Grimm? Grimm? Where are you?

Tommy Oho.

He quickly exits

Monstro appears. He is a huge, humped-backed figure with lank black hair trailing from beneath a massive turban. In the centre of this, a huge red stone gleams. Flowing sorcerer's robes trail behind him. Beside him, even Grimm looks attractive

Monstro Grimm? (*He looks round*) Bah, where is the fool? Why is he never here when I need him? No matter. I'll continue my experiments alone. (*He moves to the machine and begins to twiddle knobs and dials, all the while muttering to himself*)

Humpty backs on to the stage on a collision course with Monstro

They bump, and both turn

Humpty Oooooh. It's (*local town*)'s answer to Mr Universe.

Monstro Who are *you*?

Humpty Oh—er—I'm a *hero*.

Monstro Hero?

Humpty Yes. I saved the lives of an entire regiment of soldiers.

Monstro You *did*?

Humpty Yes. I shot the cook. (*He chortles*)

Monstro (*annoyed*) Aaaaagh. What are you doing in my secret laboratory? (*He grabs him*) Answer me. (*He shakes him violently*)

Humpty Ooo-er. I'm—I'm looking for a job. As your assistant.

Monstro Hmm. You are, are you? Well as it happens, I *do* need another pair of hands. (*He releases him*)

Humpty (*to the audience*) He's got to be joking.

Monstro Tell me, what do you know about nitrates?

Humpty Well . . . they're cheaper than *day* rates. (*He chortles*)

Monstro Fool. Imbecile. Dolt.

Humpty Here—less of the name-calling, you. There's nothing of the fool about me. I went to Oxford, I did.

Monstro *You* went to *Oxford*? (*He laughs harshly*) What did you read? English?

Humpty No. Gas meters. (*He chortles*) Here—I like your washing ma-chine. (*He indicates the machine*)

Monstro (*outraged*) Washing machine? *That* is my fantastic transforma-tion machine. With the aid of that, I can turn anyone into anything I want. Watch. (*He signals, off*)

Guards enter pushing Prisoners in chains

Into the machine with them.

Prisoners are pushed through the "In" arch and vanish

Monstro turns the wheel c

Clockwork Dolls of various kinds emerge from the "Out" arch

(*Triumphantly*) See?

He signals and the Dolls begin to dance jerkily. At the end of the dance they freeze for the applause. Monstro signals for them to go

The Dolls exit followed by the Guards

And now for my most recent arrivals. (*He calls*) Grimm. Bring in the prisoners.

Grimm enters with Mary and Polly

He sees Humpty who has not had time to move, and, swiftly drawing his sword, Grimm menaces him

Grimm Ahaaaaa. (*To Monstro*) It's Humpty Dumpty.

Monstro What? (*He whirls on Humpty*) Kill him.

Humpty Oooooooh.

Polly Run, Humpty. Run.

Humpty dashes off in panic

Monstro (*furious*) After him.

Grimm hurries off in pursuit

(*Snarling*) He won't get far. No-one has ever escaped from this castle. (*He leers at Mary*) Well, my charming poppet. It's taken quite a while to get you here, hasn't it? Though I must say it's been well worth the wait. (*He holds out his hand to touch her*)

Mary (*backing in disgust*) Keep your hands off me, you disgusting mon-ster.

Monstro (*laughing*) Monster, eh? All the same, my dear, before this night is out, you'll find yourself quite unable to resist my charms—or suffer the consequences.

Mary (*clinging to Polly*) We're not afraid of *you*.

Monstro That's what all the others said—*to begin with*. It didn't take me

long to change their minds. Now then, are you going to marry me willingly, or do you want to share their fate?

Mary I'll *never* marry you, you repulsive looking object.

Monstro (*annoyed*) Very well, then. Into the machine with you. (*He indicates*)

Tommy quickly bounds on to the stage, sword in hand

Tommy Not so fast, Monstro.

Mary and Polly utter cries of delight. Monstro turns to face Tommy

Now, Jack. Now.

Jack bounds out at the other side of Monstro

Monstro (*startled*) What? (*He quickly raises his hands to the jewel in his turban*) By the power of this jewel, I command you to drop your swords.

The Lights flicker and both Tommy and Jack drop their swords

So—try to destroy me, would you? You'll suffer for this.

Jack All right, Monstro. Do your worst. But you won't always be the winner.

Monstro (*leering*) You think not, eh? (*He laughs harshly*) With the aid of this machine and my magical jewel, no-one—but no-one—can stop my plan to rule the universe. With a single nod of my head I can bring the entire country to its *knees*.

Dame Dobb and King Florimund enter

Dame Aha. There speaks the leader of the TUC.

Monstro (*startled*) What? (*He sees them*) Who are *you*?

King Sam and Janet.

Monstro Sam and Janet who?

King (*singing*) Sam and Janet evening . . . you will see a stranger . . .

Monstro (*annoyed*) Aaaaagh. What are you doing in my enchanted castle?

Dame Well, I'll tell you. But first of all, I must warn you, I charge ten pounds for two questions.

Monstro *Ten pounds?* Isn't that rather expensive?

Dame *I* don't think so. Now what's your *second* question? (*She chortles*)

Monstro (*fuming*) You old idiot . . .

King Here. Don't you call the old idiot an old idiot. She's going to be the future Queen of Nursery-rhyme Land, she is.

Dame Yes, I am. I wasn't *going* to say "yes", but he managed to squeeze it out of me. (*She simpers*)

Monstro Bah. You're not going to be queen of anywhere, you old harridan. In five minutes time, you'll be *dead*. (*He puts his hands to the jewel*) By the power of this jewel, I . . .

Humpty comes rushing on, looking over his shoulder, and bumps heavily into Monstro, causing the turban to fly off his head

Aaaagh.

Swiftly, Tommy and Jack snatch up their swords

Grimm. Grimm. Guards.

Humpty grabs the turban and skips out of Monstro's reach

Grimm and two Guards rush on, swords drawn

Jack and Tommy fight with them. Monstro chases Humpty round the machine and the others cheer him on

·Powder and Shott hurry in carrying a large arrow-sign marked "DE-TOUR" or "DIVERSION" and stand by the "In" door of the machine

Humpty dives under the sign as he runs round the machine

Monstro sees the sign, reads it, then dashes through the "In" arch and vanishes

Powder and Shott cross the arch as Humpty jumps up and spins the wheel. There is a loud wail from inside the machine and all react. Jack and Tommy have killed the Guards and Tommy's sword is at Grimm's throat. Grimm drops his sword and cowers

Grimm (*pleading*) Mercy, mercy. (*He falls to his knees*)
Dame (*looking into the "Out" arch*) Oooooh. Look what's happened to Monstro. (*She stoops and lifts a small clockwork figure from the machine. This should be wound up already, and, displayed on the palm of her hand, the figure will clatter*)

All congratulate each other

Mother Goose enters

Mother Goose (*beaming*) Well *done*, Jack and Thomas—and Humpty too.
    You've fought your battle, good and true.
    No trace of Monstro's power remains,
    And all his victims loose their chains.

All Dolls and Prisoners come running on to cries of delight

    Now back to the Land of Nursery-rhyme,
    For the joyous end to our pantomime. (*She raises her spoon*)
Dame Here. Just a minute. Aren't you forgetting something?
King Yes. What about *him*. (*He indicates Grimm*)
Jack We can't have him running around loose.
Humpty I know. Let's ask the kids out there what to do with him.
Tommy Good idea. What shall we do with him, kids?

Audience participation whilst Grimm grovels

Mary (*laughing*) What a bloodthirsty lot of friends you've got, Humpty.
Polly There doesn't seem to be one of them with a good word for him.
Dame (*darkly*) *I've* got a good word for him—but I'm not telling you what it is.

Powder (*indicating Shott*) We've got a suggestion, haven't we, Shott?
Shott Yes. Make him watch (*particularly bad TV programme*) for the rest of his life.
Grimm (*anguished*) No. No. Anything but that. (*He grovels*)
Mother Goose So be it, then.
Now off to the palace without delay,
And we'll meet again on the wedding day.

Everyone cheers

Black-out

SCENE 6

A Corridor in the King's Palace

The Lights come up full

Humpty enters

Humpty Hiya, kids. Cor, isn't it smashing? I've got my magic powers back and everything in Nursery-rhyme Land is just as it used to be. Well . . . nearly everything. Tommy and Mary are going to get married and Dame Dobb's engaged to King Florimund, but me . . . You'll never guess what's happened to *me*. They've put me in charge of the *royal choir* and it's my job to make sure that everybody's in good voice for the wedding. Of course, there is *one* problem. As Nursery-rhyme Land is only a little country, we haven't got many people in the choir, so I want *you* to help us out. Will you do that? Right. Well I'll sing the first verse —just to show you how it's done—and then you join in the second. All right?

SONG 12 (Song sheet)

Powder and Shott, wearing their Finale costumes, enter at the end of the second verse or the second time through

Powder What on earth was that dreadful noise?
Shott It sounded like a cat with its tail under a steamroller.

Humpty, Powder and Shott discuss the merits of the audience's singing. Finally the audience is divided up and a contest ensues. For the very last repeat the song is performed by everyone

Powder, Shott and Humpty exit at the end of the song

The Lights fade quickly to Black-out

SCENE 7

The Great Ballroom and Finale

The Lights come up full on the staircase, pillars and arches of the great ball-room

As the Finale music begins the cast walk down in the following order

Babes
Choristers
Monstro
Mother Goose
Powder and Shott
Polly and Jack
Grimm
King Florimund
Dame Dobb
Humpty Dumpty
Tommy and Mary

The music stops

Mary Our pantomime is over. The time has come to part.
Tommy We hope we've brought great cheer and warmth
To each and every heart.
Dame And in the years that lie ahead—
Who knows?—you may recall
King The pleasure you all shared with us
On the night of Humpty's fall.

There is a reprise of any bright song from the show

CURTAIN

FURNITURE AND PROPERTY LIST

ACT I

PROLOGUE

On stage: Nil

Personal: **Mother Goose:** wooden spoon (used throughout)

SCENE 1

On stage: High stone wall with large arch L. *On top of wall:* huge egg
2 sentry boxes either side of arch
Palace cut out with practical door

Off stage: Simple fishing rod, short stick with several fish attached **(Tommy)**
Polystyrene eggshell shards **(Stage-management)**
Muskets or swords **(Powder** and **Shott)**

SCENE 2

On stage: Tree cut outs (optional)

Off stage: Stem rose **(Mother Goose)**

SCENE 3

On stage: Tree cut outs. *On branches:* silver bells
Flowerbeds. *In them:* flowers, plants and cockle-shells
Small rustic bench down R

SCENE 4

On stage: Nil

SCENE 5

On stage: Throne R of staircase

Off stage: Scroll **(Page)**

SCENE 6

On stage: Nil

SCENE 7

On stage: Nil

ACT II

SCENE 1

On stage: Haywain L
Haystacks R

Off stage: Bag of coins **(Grimm)**
Covered basket. *In it:* small pie **(Dame Dobb)**
Rope **(Humpty, Girls)**
2 blankets **(Powder** and **Shott)**

SCENE 2

On stage: Nil
Off stage: Cudgel **(Humpty)**
Swords **(Tommy** and **Jack)**

SCENE 3

On stage: 2 burning torches either side of door
Tree cut outs down L and R
Off stage: Tambourines **(Gypsies)**
Swords **(Tommy** and **Jack)**
Cudgel **(Humpty)**
Sword **(Grimm)**

SCENE 4

On stage: Nil
Personal: **Polly** and **Mary:** blankets
Grimm: weeds

SCENE 5

On stage: Large throne C
Off stage: Swords **(Tommy** and **Jack)**
Swords **(2 Guards)**
Large arrow sign **(Powder** and **Shott)**
Small clockwork figure—wound up **(Dame Dobb)**
Personal: **Prisoners:** chains
Grimm: sword in scabbard

SCENE 6

On stage: Song sheet or as required

SCENE 7

On stage: Full set as required

LIGHTING PLOT

Property fittings required: vari-coloured lights on transformation machine
Several simple internal and external settings

ACT I

To open: Effect of misty, early-morning light downstage

Cue 1	As **Mother Goose** waves the wooden spoon *Change to general sunny exterior lighting with spot on egg*	(Page 2)
Cue 2	As **Mary** exits *Dim lighting*	(Page 5)
Cue 3	As **Grimm** enters *Green spot on* **Grimm**	(Page 5)
Cue 4	As **Dame Dobb** enters *Bring up lighting slightly*	(Page 5)
Cue 5	**Grimm** exits *Fade green spot*	(Page 6)
Cue 6	**Dame Dobb** exits *Dim lighting slightly*	(Page 6)
Cue 7	**Mother Goose**: ". . . on the coping again." *Lights flicker gently*	(Page 7)
Cue 8	**Mother Goose**: ". . . *the egg's coming down.*" *Lights flicker madly then Black-out*	(Page 7)
Cue 9	**Humpty**: "Where am I?" *Slowly bring up general lighting*	(Page 7)
Cue 10	**Humpty**: ". . . I was miles away." *Black-out. When ready bring up general lighting slowly*	(Page 13)
Cue 11	**King** totters towards the palace *Fade to Black-out*	(Page 13)
Cue 12	To open SCENE 2 *Bring up dappled lighting effect*	(Page 13)
Cue 13	As **Grimm** enters *Green spot on* **Grimm**. *Fade as he hides*	(Page 15)
Cue 14	**Grimm** emerges from hiding *Green spot on* **Grimm**	(Page 17)
Cue 15	**Grimm** dashes off *Black-out*	(Page 18)
Cue 16	To open SCENE 3 *Bring up lighting to give a silhouette effect*	(Page 18)

Cue 17	**Mary:** ". . . all in a row." *Increase to full general lighting*	(Page 18)
Cue 18	**Grimm** enters from the garden *Green spot on Grimm*	(Page 23)
Cue 19	**Grimm** exits *Black-out*	(Page 24)
Cue 20	To open SCENE 4 *Bring up full lighting on downstage area*	(Page 24)
Cue 21	**Humpty** and the **Babes** exit happily *Fade to Black-out. When ready bring up full general lighting*	(Page 26)
Cue 22	**Grimm** enters *Green spot on **Grimm**. Fade as he exits*	(Page 27)
Cue 23	Crack of thunder *Lights flicker*	(Page 30)
Cue 24	Terrible crash *Black-out*	(Page 30)
Cue 25	**Humpty:** "Alectrician? (*More timidly*) Hello?" *Very slow fade up on **Humpty***	(Page 30)
Cue 26	**Mother Goose** enters *Misty spot on **Mother Goose***	(Page 30)
Cue 27	**Mother Goose** waves her spoon *Bring up lighting upstage to give effect of cold white with ice-blue shadow. Project snow wheel (optional). Fade misty spot on **Mother Goose** as she exits*	(Page 31)

ACT II

To open:	Effect of bright spring morning sunshine	
Cue 28	**Grimm** appears *Green spot on **Grimm**. Fade as he exits*	(Page 34)
Cue 29	**Grimm** emerges from behind haystack *Green spot on **Grimm**. Fade as he exits*	(Page 34)
Cue 30	**Grimm** enters stealthily *Green spot on **Grimm***	(Page 38)
Cue 31	All exit *Black-out*	(Page 38)
Cue 32	To open SCENE 2 *Bring up gloomy lighting on downstage area*	(Page 38)
Cue 33	**Mother Goose** waves her spoon *Lights flicker*	(Page 39)
Cue 34	All exit *Black-out*	(Page 40)
Cue 35	To open SCENE 3 *Bring up effect of blue, green and red lighting on **Gypsies***	(Page 40)
Cue 36	**Grimm** appears in the doorway *Green spot on **Grimm**. Fade as he exits*	(Page 41)

Cue 37	**Dame Dobb** shrugs *Black-out*	(Page 43)
Cue 38	To open SCENE 4 *Bring up interior lighting on downstage area*	(Page 43)
Cue 39	**Grimm** enters *Green spot on* **Grimm.** *Fade as he exits*	(Page 44)
Cue 40	**Grimm** enters *Green spot on* **Grimm**	(Page 45)
Cue 41	**Grimm** pulls the girls off stage *Fade to Black-out*	(Page 45)
Cue 42	To open SCENE 5 *Bring up interior lighting*	(Page 45)
Cue 43	**Monstro** twiddles knobs and dials on machine *Vari-coloured lights on machine begin flashing*	(Page 46)
Cue 44	**Grimm** enters *Green spot on* **Grimm.** *Fade as he exits*	(Page 47)
Cue 45	**Monstro:** ". . . to drop your swords." *Lights flicker*	(Page 48)
Cue 46	**Grimm** enters *Green spot on* **Grimm**	(Page 49)
Cue 47	Everyone cheers *Black-out*	(Page 50)
Cue 48	To open SCENE 6 *Bring up full interior lighting on downstage area with spot on song sheet*	(Page 50)
Cue 49	**Powder, Shott** and **Humpty** exit *Quick fade to Black-out*	(Page 50)
Cue 50	To open SCENE 7 *Bring up to full general lighting*	(Page 50)

EFFECTS PLOT

ACT I

MADE AND PRINTED IN GREAT BRITAIN BY
LATIMER TREND & COMPANY LTD PLYMOUTH

MADE IN ENGLAND